# THE RAILWAYS OF MANCHESTER

## C. T. Goode

1986

ISBN 0/9508239/8/8

72 Woodland Drive, Anlaby, Hull. HU10 7HX.

# Contents

# Introduction

In this compact and, I hope, readable history of the railways serving Manchester I have endeavoured to cover every aspect of development in as logical a way as possible, not always easy where old companies overlap, as in the Stalybridge area. However, with the aid of the table of contents the reader should soon find the particular section required. There has of late been a miniature deluge of books on Manchester's railways, and I commend several of these which often cover a particular facet of the history in far more detail than would be possible within these pages. Faults there will surely be, and readers will no doubt rush to correct them; however, as well as accuracy I have striven for the re-creation of atmosphere such as that once found on Bury's stations, at rambling Rochdale or at Guide Bridge when the place was all intact, preferably savoured on a wet and murky day when steam was supreme.

I cannot acknowledge every source of assistance here, but mention my enjoyment in looking up all the standard company histories and assistance freely given by library staff at Bolton, Manchester, Stockport and Stalybridge, among others.

Criticism of all kinds is welcomed, as are suggestions for subjects on similar works to which I could turn my attention in future.

C. Tony Goode BA

Anlaby, Hull. 1986

# Abbreviations

| | |
|---|---|
| L & MR | Liverpool and Manchester Railway |
| L & BR | London and Birmingham Railway |
| B & LR | Bolton and Leigh Railway |
| G Jc. R | Grand Junction Railway |
| M & Ch. Jc. | Manchester and Chester Jc. Railway |
| LNWR | London and North Western Railway |
| L & YR | Lancashire and Yorkshire Railway |
| SA & MR | Sheffield, Ashton and Manchester Railway |
| MS & LR | Manchester, Sheffield and Lincolnshire Railway |
| GCR | Great Central Railway |
| MS Jc. & AR | Manchester, South Jc. and Altrincham Railway |
| M & LR | Manchester and Leeds Railway |
| OA &GBR | Oldham, Ashton and Guide Bridge Railway |
| ELR | East Lancashire Railway |
| MSCR | Manchester Ship Canal Railway |

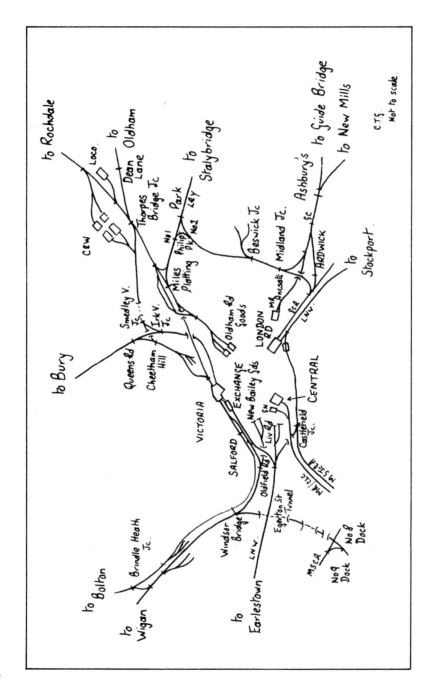

The Industrial Revolution made possibly its greatest impact upon Manchester and Liverpool and their environs, where little unpretentious villages suddenly found themselves with great mill blocks or vast holes in the ground providing employment for workpeople who came to seek jobs and then settled in. By the end of the nineteenth century the population of Liverpool had more than doubled, only exceeded in miraculous growth by Manchester and Salford. Cotton was imported from the New World in ever increasing amounts, to be returned there in due course as finished goods for sale. The thriving port of Liverpool also handled a growing amount of emigrant traffic. The world was indeed active, with labour, work and commodities in good supply. The bulk of commercial traffic was carried by canal, and the Leeds & Liverpool had been built with this very aim in mind and successfully linked the abovementioned cities.

In 1804 the Rochdale canal was opened from Manchester along the Calder valley, reaching 610 ft. without the need for any tunnel. At this time Manchester was the focal point of the cotton trade, and by 1834 about one half of the finished products was exported by way of Liverpool, Goole or Hull, taking up to a week along the canal to reach the latter port. The new turnpike roads could also be utilised, with carts bringing loads to Selby which were then transhipped to steam packets on the Ouse to Hull.

At this time there was no polarisation of wool or cotton processing. The popular idea that Lancashire was for cotton and Yorkshire was for wool only grew with the railways when zoning of manufacture was a simple convenience. In 1830 quite a number of cotton mills could be found in the West Riding.

In 1790 the Manchester, Bolton & Bury canal was constructed, adapted after a time to take the wider Leeds & Liverpool boats. On this canal a packet boat conveyed passengers between Bolton and Manchester for 1/6 return from about 1796. Canals were usually reliable but suffered from slowness and frequent congestion, so that entrepreneurs looked to the new railway ideas as a way of speeding things up and keeping abreast of what would nowadays be called 'modern technology.' The first whisper of a railway in the area under review would link up Manchester with Liverpool, and its very idea unleashed a torrent of hostility from vested interests such as canal and land owners and thoses who administered turnpike tolls.

The line of route of the Liverpool & Manchester Railway was relatively simple, apart from the extremities and some soggy terrain, and was surveyed by William James, a Midlands lawyer and mineowner, and Joseph Sandars, a Liverpool businessman. The line was in essence a Liverpool project and was authorised by its Act of 5th May 1826 to run to Salford and then, by a further Act of 15th May to cross the Irwell to a terminus at Liverpool Road.

The line was engineered by George Stephenson and John Rennie, though the latter withdrew after a year due to some dispute or other. In view of what later transpired it is interesting to record that there was initial opposition to free running engines and that fixed haulage machines were preferred. One was installed for the Edge Hill incline in Liverpool. However, reason prevailed and the Rainhill Trials were allowed to become a worthy part of history. Much has been written about the event and some of the facts have been well and truly embroidered, much as those old prints have which render cutting walls and tunnels larger than life. The Trials were discovered some time ago by the Author as prescribed reading in German primary schools - no harm here as long as the practices therein are not assumed to reflect current BR policy!

*Two fine ex GC tank engines grace the LNER side of London Road.    H. C. Casserley*

The facts are these: A prize of £500 was awarded to the best locomotive to perform on the trial stretch of double track at Rainhill, the contest to be held on 6th October 1829. Four locomotives entered and were called upon to run up and down forty times on a section 1¾ miles long which equalled the total length between Manchester and Liverpool and back. The speed was not to exceed 10 mph. and a measured tonnage was to be hauled in proportion to the weight of the engine. In the middle of various strange devices, only the 'Rocket' proved its worth and was deemed to have won. After running-in sessions the line was officially opened on 15th September 1830 when eight trains left Liverpool watched by many thousands of spectators. Stephenson drove 'Northumbrian' at the head of a train of worthies including the Duke of Wellington, travelling on the 'wrong' or right hand line, while the more plebian trains ran on the customary left.

At Parkside the 'Northumbrian' halted for water and while it was occupied Mr. William Huskisson got down on to the track to stretch his legs and was run over by the 'Rocket' coming along parallel in charge of the third train. Thus the gentleman ensured his inclusion in the record books as the first railway accident victim. 'Northumbrian' took him on to Eccles in the leading coach, while the rest was hauled by chain from the adjacent line until 'Northumbrian' could return to it. The accident cast a shadow on the festive day, the crowds lining the route were less vociferous and the buffet at Liverpool Road station, fortunately cold, was not so greatly enjoyed. The Duke of Wellington did not even leave his coach but asked to see Huskisson, a move which was not possible because of the immense crowds. Eventually he left the train at Roby after an eventful and certainly memorable day. Today a monument marking the incident survives at the lineside. The accident no doubt increased public curiousity in the new means of transport and cheap excursions were soon run, with regular passenger services from 19th September and goods workings from 1st December 1830.

Much has been made of the Liverpool Road station, perhaps because it managed to survive for so long and has been restored. It was far from impressive with a pseudo-classical facade and stairs up from street level to the single platform. However, it is generally acknowledged to be the oldest passenger station in the country.

The first stations in the Manchester area were Cross Lane, Eccles and Patricroft, with the later addition of Weaste Lane.

The Liverpool and Manchester could well exist independently with the vast amount of local traffic generated; however, plans were already laid for links with the outside world which would bring the two cities nearer to the rest of the country.

Getting to Bolton was one of the first priorities, and with this aim in mind the Bolton and Leigh Railway was constructed and opened to goods traffic in 1828, to be followed by the L & MR sponsored Kenyon & Leigh Junction Railway which met the former head-on, opened for goods traffic in January

*A 2P leaving Manchester Cen. on a Midland working.*                    *H. C. Casserley*

1831 and to passengers in the following summer. Kenyon Junction was an odd place, one of those sprawling railway oases without any visible town or village to back them up, as here, where traffic could be interchanged. The junction trailed in towards Liverpool and there were a couple of workings running through to Leigh and Bolton Great Moor Street station from the outset. The line was nominally independent until 1846 and services ran through to Liverpool with additional excursion workings. Private wagons were run to and from Kenyon and private locomotives could be operated on the running lines as well. Enterprise was the key work here. By 1843 the Bolton & Leigh had seen excursions to London complete with overnight lodgings included in a vintage 'mini-break deal' for £2.18s.6d. Both the lines were to be taken over by the London & North Western.

West of Manchester and on the north-south axis the Grand Junction Railway was opened from Warrington to Birmingham in 1837 and so traffic could be generated via Newton Jc. between London and the Liverpool Road station over the L & MR. Liverpool Road was suitably extended as a result. The main section of trunk route from Birmingham to London Euston, the London and Birmingham was opened on 19th September 1838, while the L & MR was absorbed by the Grand Junction one year earlier. The two of them became part of the LNWR in 1846.

*Kenyon Jc. (LNWR). Line on left to Bolton Great Moor St.*      *R. M. Casserley*

The Grand Junction way of travelling between Manchester and London via Warrington was considered to be too circuitous and a more direct route southwards from Manchester was planned, in fact two principal schemes were mooted in the 1830s, firstly the Manchester & Cheshire Junction which would run directly via Stockport to the Grand Junction at Crewe Hall, and the

*Loco No. 41215 at Bolton, Great Moor St.*                    *H. C. Casserley*

Manchester South Union which would run through the Potteries and Lichfield to the Birmingham and Derby line at Tamworth from which place a branch would run to Rugby. The Grand Junction naturally supported the Cheshire Junction scheme as it involved them and would be financially advantageous. The other scheme was regarded as being too roundabout. The M & B was a compromise between two schemes as finally carried out, with the line running through the Potteries with a branch to Crewe. As history later showed, the latter branch became the main line and the section of route between Macclesfield and Cheadle became the lesser line.

On 4th June 1840 the first section of the Manchester and Birmingham opened from a terminus in Travis Street, Manchester, not far from the site of the later Mayfield station, running through one station at Rushford (Longsight) to a station on the north side of the Mersey at Stockport, opened as a temporary terminus on the first day. Rushford closed early, in April 1843 and was replaced by Longsight. Heaton Chapel station opened in January 1852, while Levenshulme had opened ten years earlier.

The impressive, tall viaduct at Stockport, 600 yd. long and 111 ft. high was completed on 21st December 1840 and ceremoniously opened, allowing the line to run west of the town to Sandbach, which it did from 10th May 1842. A station was provided at Cheadle which became Cheadle Hulme. South of the Stockport viaduct a temporary station was built at Edgeley, opened on 15th February 1843 and deemed unsuccessful after a few weeks, not because of its obviously convenient location, but because of one of those familiar bureaucratic quirks which in this case let only the local trains stop there while the Crewe fast trains passed through. They did call at the original station north of the river, now named Heaton Norris. Omnibuses ran up Warren Hill to this station and travellers soon preferred to go on to Manchester directly by road rather than have the fuss of a change. However, reason prevailed, a reprieve was granted and Edgeley came to stay. The Crewe trains had run from 10th August 1842, as well as a service to Chester. Travis Street closed very soon after the line opened, and London Road, often known as Bank Top or Store Street took over, with its two platforms and six storage lines linked by turntables between them.

There had been several schemes to link up Manchester with the area south of the Mersey stretching along towards the Wirral, some of them going back to 1835. Prominent among such schemes was the Birkenhead, Lancs. and Cheshire Junction Railway, by which an Act of June 1846 proposed a line from Hooton to Heaton Norris and a branch to the Manchester, South Junction and Altrincham at Timperley. There were objections from the Grand Junction who saw the competition for traffic between Stockport and Warrington, where, in any case there would be congestion due to the tricky terrain which prevented any widening on embankments. Initially the line opened for passengers on 18th December 1850, with three trains each way between Manchester Victoria and Chester and connections for Ireland. Some relief was given to Warrington by a line from Warrington Arpley, east of the main line north-south, to Timperley and then to Stockport, a route opened throughout in November 1853 as far as Broadheath station, Altrincham. Delay in the construction of river bridges prevented full working until May 1854, when stations at Latchford, Lymm and Heatley were opened en route. Thelwall, Warburton and Dunham were to follow later. Heatley became Heatley and Warburton and Dunham became Dunham Massey.

The line is interesting in that it was an 'alternative route', rather unwanted and treated as such by the LNWR who moderated the Warrington-Manchester traffic coming this way and imposed tariffs on it. Goods trains were usually only run at night, not in itself a bad thing. Beyond Warrington the line ran on to Garston at the east end of Liverpool's docks and this geographical fact generated interest from other companies. To begin with, the Manchester, Sheffield and Lincolnshire Railway had worked trains on the line from October 1856 and had run two express goods trains for their own traffic between Manchester and Garston up to October 1865. The Great Northern Railway, never remiss at seizing opportunities to 'poach', had put on a fast King's Cross-Garston service from February 1858. Much of this rather spectacular working ceased after 1865 when traffic returned to normal levels, in fact the LNWR took over the engine workings from the MS & L in 1860 and absorbed the Warrington & Garston in July 1864.

It is worthy of note that as early as 1839 a proposal had already been made to link up Liverpool Road station with London Road by means of a tunnel beneath the centre of the city, perhaps with a central station in Piccadilly Gardens. Railway events were also quickly shaping up on the other side of Manchester from Stockport, but to avoid confusion those developments which affected London Road and the LNWR will be taken together. Involved here was the Sheffield, Ashton under Lyne and Manchester Railway (later MS & L), authorised on 5th May 1857 and permitted to share first Travis

*Outside Gorton Works.*                                    *C. T. Goode*

Street for its trains out to Godley to the east which started running from 17th November 1841 and then London Road as the line extended still further out to Woodhead from 8th August 1844 and right through to Sheffield from 23rd December 1845. Manchester area stations opened on the SA & M from the outset were Ardwick (January 1842), Ashbury's (July 1855) and Gorton (September 1842), resited in August 1906.

The SA & M was an interested partner in a company known as the Manchester, South Junction and Altrincham, already mentioned above, which embodied echoes of the cross-city link proposal. In 1844 the M & B and the SA & M agreed on sponsoring a line which would run from independent platforms near London Road and would lead south from the city on a long viaduct to reach the L & M line at Ordsall Lane. This proposal suited the M & B very well indeed, as they badly needed a route to the West coast. This Southern Junction line, as it became known as, was about 1½ miles in length. A branch was thrown in along with the Southern Junction, running along the Manchester-Runcorn canal which the trustees of the Bridgewater Estate wished to convert. In the event both means of transport survived cheek by jowl and the branch which ran from Castlefield Jc. on the Southern link ran for eight miles to Altrincham, becoming very important. Both lines were opened in 1849.

From 1845 up to Nationalisation in 1948 the MS Jc. & A was virtually independent, having its own directors, three from each owning company but under the owners' control. Thus the joint LMS/LNER control passed finally to the Midland Region of British Rail. The original capital raised was £400,000 and £50,000 was issued to the Bridgewater Canal Company, whose packet boats to Runcorn ceased operating once the line opened. The section of line to Altrincham opened on 21st July 1849, the remainder two months later. Money ran short, due chiefly to the construction of the long viaduct to Ordsall Lane which sported 224 arches. The Company offices were at Oxford Road, and the Chairman alternated yearly, thus causing regular changes of policy. In the end an independent member joined the Board to see fair play. In September 1849 the line extended to Bowdon which was actually the terminus until April 1881, when Altrincham was resited to become Altrincham and Bowdon. Earliest stations were Knott Mill and Deansgate, Old Trafford, Edge Lane (Stretford), Sale and Timperley. Sale enjoyed several aliases before reversion in 1931. Cornbrook closed in 1865 after about ten years, while Brooklands opened in December 1859. One particularly intriguing station was 'Manchester Art Treasures Exhibition' which opened for the season in 1857 and again in 1887 and was used for cricket and football matches.

The majority of trains was operated by the MS & L up to 1900, followed by an increase in LNWR interest up to 1923, when LMS and LNER engines worked in five year cycles. While the traffic on the Altrincham branch was chiefly commuter passenger services, that on the Southern Junction to Ordsall Lane was mainly freight, with over 100 such workings in 1899. Passenger workings here were never prominent and only a few such trains were run before 1868 to connect at Ordsall Lane with Liverpool services. At this early period a Liverpool-York night mail working could be seen taking this route before being transferred to the new CLC route via Stockport. Up to 1914 the LNWR ran a circuitous Oxford Road-Bolton Moor Street service, while there was also a Buxton-Liverpool operation and through coaches between Euston and Bolton via London Road.

More will be said about MS Jc. & A fortunes in a later chapter.


Time now to leave a fairly solid pattern of lines south and west of Manchester and to concentrate on filling in some of the railway development to the north and east. The Manchester, Bolton & Bury Canal Company was formed in 1790, first made narrow then wide to take barges off the Leeds & Liverpool canal and with a branch cut from near Horwich to Bolton. Freight was the main commodity, though a packet boat conveyed passengers between Bolton and Manchester for 1/6- return from 1796. In August 1831 an Act authorised the conversion of the canal to railway in order to pre-empt other schemes which were seeking funds, through advertising in local newspapers. The name of the company now became the Bolton & Bury Canal Navigation & Railway Company and it was decided that the canal would continue to work until one line was ready for use. Estimates were given by Nimmo who was succeeded by Jesse Hartley after his untimely death. Hartley recommended that the canal be retained and that three lines should be laid from the outset. Work started from the Salford end in June 1833. The Manchester & Bolton Works and a two road shed were placed west of Salford station on the south side of the line between Ordsall Lane and Oldfield Road, adjacent to the canal.

As mentioned, the Bolton & Leigh Railway had been opened in 1828 and overtures had been made by both companies for a union without, however, any progress being achieved. Engineering works, now in the hands of John Hawkshaw, proved more expensive than anticipated and doubled the cost quoted of £600,000 before completion in February 1838. The terrain was a tricky mixture of wet sand and clay with much high embankment and the 295yd. long tunnel at Farnworth, a noteworthy bridge at Kearsley and two others at Farnworth and Moses Gate. There was a cutting at Pepper Hill which touched 101 ft. in depth and three embankments varying in height from 44 to 67 ft. In places the canal ran parallel to the railway, being often higher by as much as 27ft. as at Clifton, where it was held by robust retaining walls. The Salford terminus was on a low viaduct, 444 yd. long with 38 arches, while the station itself was 78 ft. long and 30ft. wide, facing New Bailey Street. The terminus at Bolton was on the flat with five lines, each ending in a turntable sited between Bridgeman Street and Trinity Street. There was one narrow island platform. Engines could be attended to at both ends of the line. The formation did allow for the three running lines, except at tunnels, though only two lines were ever provided. One curious fact of operation until September 1846 was that of right hand running, said to be safer for trains from Bolton which could descend the 1 in 200 on the steeper right hand side of the valley and which, if derailed, would fall across the other line and not topple off the embankment. The first rain of maroon firsts and blue seconds, all of course four wheelers, ran on 17th May 1838 out from Salford and return. The total original coaching stock was 37 and all must have been in use in the make-up of the two trains hauled by 'Bolton' and 'Fairfield' which conveyed passengers on that glorious day.

*Farnworth station on the L & Y line to Bolton. Hardly anything of the buildings survives today.*                                                    *Bolton Public Libraries*

Rumour had it that the level of comfort was superior to that on the L & M trains. Third class was introduced, to be suspended for a short time when it proved too popular at 1/- return. By January 1847 the Bolton line had 18 first class, 25 seconds and 14 third class carriages. There were stations at Agecroft Bridge (3 miles), Ringley (7 miles), Dixon Fold (Clifton) (5 miles) and Pendleton (Windsor Bridge) (1 mile), closed in 1846 and later replaced by a station further out, Farnworth (8¼ miles) and Moses Gate (8½ miles). The names of some of the stations varied over the years; Ringley was Kearsley and Farnworth had four variations.

An accident did take place on the line, though not on an embankment as feared, but in cutting at Clifton on 4th March 1853 when a Bury 0-4-0 broke an axle, bringing eight coaches off the road with it and killing the crew and two passengers. The contemporary account of the event mentions looting of the carriages by local residents.

Regular interval departures ran from each end of the line at 8, 9, 12, 3, 5 and 7 hours, with two trains on Sundays. Rather unusually, the passenger services began before goods workings were introduced.

Near to Dixon Fold station at the west end a branch left to serve three collieries in the vicinity, leading to sidings on the south side. Part of the run was by way of a 1 in 5 incline which was rope worked from opening on 30th April 1840. On one occasion a wagon broke loose, flew across the main line, took flight and landed a good distance away at the foot of the embankment. After this display a zig-zag incline was laid, later to be graced by the little electric shunting engines from Kearsley power station. In March 1878 another branch of just over one mile was opened from Kearsley to serve more collieries near Walkden, and this too had a gradient, though only 1 in 50. The line was either constructed by a single navvy or financed on a day to day basis, as it took four years to complete!

The Rochdale canal route was followed by the Manchester & Leeds Railway, formed in 1825. George Stephenson and James Walker surveyed a line which, originally, was planned to leave the L & M and run across the northern part of the city by way of Hulme, Ardwick and Newton. There was the statutory opposition from the Canal company who conveyed the stone, grain and general cargo in a slow but certain way. At the third attempt the Bill was passed on 4th July 1836, proposing a route of 51 miles which would climb for ten miles to a tunnel and run to Normanton where running powers could be exercised over the North Midland line to Leeds. If the latter line were unfinished, then the Manchester and Leeds could finish it for them. The younger brother of the famous Great Western locomotive engineer, Thomas Gooch, gained the task of constructing the line, though he had plenty on his hands with the completion of Kilsby tunnel on the London and Birmingham. An Act of May 1837 modified plans somewhat and on 18th August 1837 work began at Rochdale and at the terminus at Manchester Oldham Road which was built on a viaduct to ease the gradient. Here was a large building 176 yd. by 80 yd. of three storeys and with a booking office at ground level, opened in 1839. In the manner of St. Pancras space was available beneath to store goods, wagons being lowered by hoist until a 1 in 27 incline was put in during 1874. In spite of the viaduct there was still a tidy pull of 1 in 150 up to Miles Platting where the engine shed was situated.

The line was opened promptly at midday on 3rd July 1839 as far as Littleborough, the gradients demanding the use of two little 0-4-2 engines in tandem on each of the two trains; thus 'Stephenson' and 'Kenyon', 'Stanley' and 'Lancaster' took out eleven coach trains along the thirteen mile stretch which was now open to the public. Thousands came along on the next day. First class was blue, while seconds were yellow with windowless shutters. The thirds were rough and revolting, with no seats.

The North Midland did manage to reach Normanton from Leeds and indeed supplied motive power on the next section of the M & L opened, from Normanton to Hebden Bridge on 5th October 1840 until the difficult middle section, which included the Summit tunnel, was opened on 1st March 1841. The first train through was the 9.20 to Normanton which then ran back the short distance to Wakefield for a presentation lunch in honour of Thomas Gooch.

Summit tunnel is 1 mile 1,125 yd. long and at the time of its opening was the first to carry a railway line across the Pennines. Fourteen shafts were sunk, to enable work to go ahead from thirty faces. Cost was £300,000, and 23 million bricks as well as 8,000 tons of cement were used in its construction. The durability of the thick lining of the tunnel was put to a cruel test just prior to Christmas 1984 when a train of tanker wagons was derailed therein, catching fire and causing a great blaze which used several of the shafts as handy roaring chimneys for a time. This caused closure of the tunnel until the following May, until which time trains ran to Todmorden and Littleborough on either side and a bus link filled the gap. The solid construction work of over a century earlier had stood abuse extremely well.

Initially there were 8 or 9 trains each way between Leeds and Manchester, and 4 trains on Sundays. Stations were provided at Mills Hill for Oldham (5½ miles), Heywood Blue Pitts (7¾) and Rochdale.

A certain Thomas Edmonson had come from the Newcastle and Carlisle to be Chief Booking Clerk at Oldham Road, bringing with him a new machine which was able to print, number and date the tickets. The idea was adopted by the M & L along with a system of coding and marking the card tickets to prevent fiddling. The Edmonson system became standard for very many years.

On the other side of the Pennines Normanton was now important as a junction, its status enhanced even further when the York and North Midland opened its line from there to York, with access to Leeds via Milford Jc. and through there via Selby to Hull from July 1840. These resorts were now available to the M & L via Normanton, though not of course to the L & M who sought to fill in the gap between their own station and Oldham Road. A proposal was made, therefore, to build a line from Miles Platting, through a station at Hunts Bank and along a sinuous link to the L & M. The Hunts Bank site was acquired for the M & L by its vice chairman and handed over privately in August 1838. The M & L would build the section from Miles Platting, the M & B the central portion and the L & M the western end, following the Act of 14th June 1839. The M & L Act was passed one month later and included a branch to Oldham. All was not plain sailing, as the Duke of Bridgewater displayed his M & B interests by pressing for a longer and more expensively route running further south and with more road and river bridges. A fresh Act of 30th July 1842 confirmed the more reasonable proposal which saved some £250,000 on the dearer estimate and up to one thousand yards in length.

17

*An L & Y 2-4-2 T backed by the impressive hulk of Manchester Victoria.*     *H. C. Casserley*

*Old L & YR passenger engine retains its old livery at Victoria in June 1926.*     *H. C. Casserley*

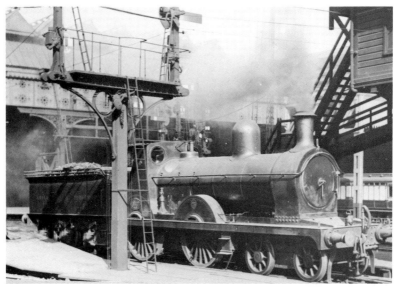

To take the M & L side of things first. Under the general eye of Gooch, Brogden the contractor commenced work on his section of line, just over two miles, in June 1842, and 2,320 yd. were on heavy gradients of 1 in 47 and 1 in 59 into Hunts Bank. A station was tendered for Hunts Bank for £19,000 and there was to be another at Miles Platting at the top end, where a 240 hp. stationary engine was placed. The line opened on 1st January 1844, and Oldham Road closed after about four years. Brogden had to supply some quite impressive engineering pieces in close proximity to each other, beginning with a fifty yard viaduct, then a 433 yd. embankment, a cutting almost as long and a 38 arch viaduct over the Irk. Rope haulage was soon discontinued when it was found that the engines could cope; one 0-4-2 became an 0-6-0 and acted as pilot.

As might be expected, Hunts Bank station was called Victoria, though to be accurate, after the Victoria bridge over the Irwell which was opened in 1839. The Victoria station was the largest in the country at the time of its completion. Trains left from each end of one single platform of 852 ft. which was almost entirely roofed over. There were five tracks which were linked centrally by a double row of turntables. Offices were contained in a building 266 ft. by 36 ft. and the respective companies inhabited each end with the important refreshment facilities in the middle. The frontage was Roman Doric in style.

The L & M section was ready in July 1843 and included a nine foot cast iron screen at one side at the Salford end to keep the view of the New Bailey prison away from delicate passengers. After passing alongside Salford station the line crossed the Irwell by a bridge 12 ft. long. The lines were laid and the whole was opened to traffic from 4th May 1844. After two years some Bolton services began to use Victoria. The section of line out to Rochdale from Victoria was developed tremendously from the outset and contained some of the most intensively used running lines, with attendant signalling, to be found anywhere. The M & L was soon to become the Lancashire and Yorkshire Railway, a proud company and one which remained independent of any direct London interests. North of Victoria a relief route was put in to the west running by way of Cheetham Hill Jc., still with a climb at 1 in 63 through the 262 yd. Queens Road tunnel to Thorpes Bridge Jc. where the original line was rejoined. Passenger trains favoured the newer route, leaving the original route through Miles Platting station to the locals and freight trains, especially those bound for the Brewery Exchange Sidings or Oldham Road station, later to be the city's largest goods depot for east-west traffic.

North of Miles Platting was the shed at Newton Heath on the east side, the largest and most important on the L & Y with over two hundred engines at one period contained in 24 bays and ending its days as a steam shed with 2-6-2 and 2-6-4 tanks, 0-6-0s, Fowler 0-8-0s, 8Fs, WDs and 'Jubilees'. Opposite were the Lightbowne carriage sidings. After Moston colliery came Middleton Jc., an important place with a set of fine awnings, junction for the Middleton branch and of the branch to Oldham via Werneth, in fact Middleton Jc. when originally called Mills Hill, was the halt for Oldham before the branch was built.

Castleton station was originally called Blue Pitts and sported a triangular junction with the Bolton line running off westwards; in the centre of the layout here were sidings, latterly full of old rolling stock, not perhaps surprising as there was also a permanent way depot on the same side-such places tend to

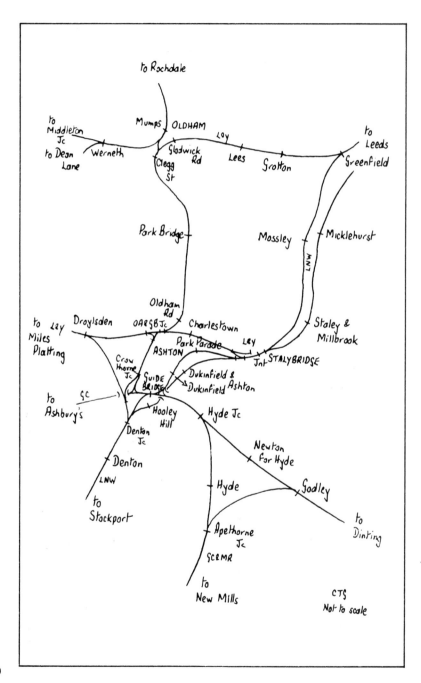

to Rochdale

to Middleton Jc
to Dean Lane
Werneth
Mumps
OLDHAM
LoY
Gladwick Rd
Clegg St
Lees
Grotton
to Leeds
Greenfield

Park Bridge

Mossley
Micklehurst
LNW

Oldham Rd
Droylsden
OA&GBJc
Charlestown
to LoY
Miles Platting
Park Parade
ASHTON
LoY
Staley & Millbrook
Crow thorne Jc
GUIDE BRIDGE
Dukinfield & Ashton
Dukinfield
Jnt STALYBRIDGE
to Ashbury's
GC
Hooley Hill
Hyde Jc
Denton Jc
Newton for Hyde
Denton
LNW
Hyde
Godley
to Stockport
Apethorne Jc
SC&MR
to Dinting
to New Mills

CTS
Not to scale

20

attract more exotic and lame vehicles. To Castleton the main line rose at 1 in 152. Rochdale was approached over a 25 arch viaduct. In its final form Rochdale station was an impressive affair with two long island platforms and four bays, two at each end.

It is now essential to retrace our steps to Victoria station, and add in the other lines which were to bring the mill towns together.

It was obviously not satisfactory to have Oldham served at long range from the main line at Middleton, and so a branch, part of the M & L Act of 1839 was surveyed from there by Stephenson and Gooch in December 1840. The contract for the construction of the line was awarded to Graham and Smith and allowed a double track climbing up an incline of 1 in 27 at Werneth, for which a 17ft. haulage wheel and rope would be used, the rising loads counterbalanced by ballasted wagons coming down on the other line of rails. There would be trains every half hour if necessary, made up of up to seven carriages or nine wagons. The rope haulage materialised and survived until about 1854.

The station at the junction was first known as Oldham Jc., then renamed Middleton in 1842, upon which Mills Hill was closed. Thereafter, from May of that year, the station became Middleton Jc. and the line to Middleton was opened on 5th January 1857. On the Oldham line, trains ran to a terminus at

*Ashton Park Parade station with manpower.*          *Heyday Publishing*

Werneth, then extended into Mumps station from 1st November 1847 (the fascinating name comes possibly from a local work meaning 'alms') and from the outset the line enjoyed a comfortable amount of traffic.

The following stages in the development of railways from Oldham were linked closely with the fortunes of Ashton-under-Lyne, a proud and well-planned old market town with a population of about 40,000, a producer of cotton goods and, like Oldham, desirous of obtaining an outlet to the west coast.

As we have seen, Oldham was now linked to the M & L by its branch from Middleton Jc. to the north. In the early days of railways Ashton, too, was left to the north of an important line, here the SA & MR running west-east, and although the town's name was part of the company title, the nearest they could manage was Guide Bridge which lay two miles outside the main area served and so inadequate, in fact it became one of those stations which appeared to exist chiefly for enthusiasts and railwaymen.

Things improved somewhat when the M & L opened their Ashton & Stalybridge Junction line which really consisted of two branches, one from Miles Platting to Stalybridge opened six months later. This somewhat meandering line of 6½ miles gave Ashton a central station of its own and ran to a terminal station at Stalybridge which was north of and hard by the later version.

Stalybridge and Ashton were served by another branch line, promoted by the SA & MR from Guide Bridge up through stations at Dukinfield and Ashton (Park Parade from 1862), to run to Stalybridge from the south west. The Act for the line allowed for an extension eastwards to Saddleworth. The branch, 2¼ miles long, was opened on 23rd December 1845 concurrent with Woodhead tunnel on the main Sheffield line, but not before 17 men had been killed in the previous April due to the collapse of a viaduct at Ashton. The line followed a sinuous and rather dingy course on arches and through sidings with somewhat Wagnerian scenery. Quite recently the motive power at Guide Bridge has been parked out on the curve adjacent to the running lines at the Guide Bridge end. The intermediate stations have vanished without trace.

The M & B, later to become part of the LNWR, now realised that if it could complete one further important part of the railway jigsaw, then it would be able to gain Stalybridge from its main Euston route and aim at securing an eventual access 'over the top' to Leeds. So, in 1845, it obtained an Act for the construction of the line from Heaton Norris to Guide Bridge via Denton, which was opened on 1st August 1849. This line was to play a vital part in linking important places to the east and north of Manchester with those round Stockport and beyond, as traffic was now able to be moved directly without passing through the city centre, due to 'connections in the right places', as recent publicity for the Slaybridge-Stockport railcar service put it. Again, the line was visually nothing to write home about, with four tracks in places and eventually stations at Reddish and Denton. Running powers were given by the M & L over the branch from Stalybridge to Manchester Victoria. Meanwhile the LNWR had been busily occupied in buying the Leeds, Dewsbury and Manchester Railway, as well as the Huddersfield and Manchester Railway and Canal Company, with the result that their line via Standedge tunnel, between Stalybridge and Huddersfield was conveniently opened on the same day as that to Heaton Norris.

Ashton station on the OA & GB Jc. Railway.                    *H. C. Casserley*

Oldham interests promoted the possibility of 24 miles of independent lines, including a separate route to Piccadilly and whispers of an extension to Merseyside. No doubt this was so much pie in the sky aimed at catching the ear of committed railway companies and driving them to take action. In the event, these District Railway proposals were diluted somewhat to become the Oldham Alliance Railway of 1846; still without any tangible results. The basic need was to connect Oldham to the LNWR and L & Y systems to the south. The LNWR obliged by opening its branch from Greenfield, east of Stalybridge, to Mumps temporary station on 5th July 1856, though trains came off in the wrong direction, that is, towards Huddersfield. A more practical solution to the problem was the joint sponsoring by the MS & L and LNWR of the Oldham, Ashton and Guide Bridge Junction Railway, which was to run the four miles from Mumps to Ashton, with a westwards facing junction with the Stalybridge branch. An interesting relic of the venture survives at the time of writing in the unusual signal box nameplate at the site 'OA & GB Jc.', which must have bothered many a passer-by. From here the line set off again, turning almost immediately south to Guide Bridge, where a triangular junction was made with the MS & L main line. The early history of the OA & GB was not without its squabbles, as the MS & L had firstly sought the L & Y as its partner, and then turned additionally to the LNWR. However, this displeased the L & Y who withdrew, though allowing passage over the few chains of their branch at Ashton. The Guide Bridge end was completed without incident in March 1860, while the trickier section north of Ashton with various embankments, tunnelling and viaducts took longer. Wet weather slowed things

23

down. There was a 56 ft. cutting near Park Bridge where there was also a 200 yd. long viaduct and a further one of 80 yd. at Limehurst. The line was opened throughout on 31st July 1861 and a passenger service operated by the MS & L from London Road to Oldham and back began on 26th August 1861, somewhat unusually before the goods service which began on 1st February 1863. The first special train left London Road at noon on 31st July 1861 carrying 200 guests.

There were stations at Ashton Moss (closed in 1862!), Ashton and Park Bridge. Werneth line trains from the L & Y ran to Central station in Oldham, while the OA & GB services ran to their own station at Clegg Street nearly opposite. There was an end-on junction with the LNWR at Glodwick Road.

The Greenfield branch trains now ran on to Clegg Street from July 1862, and the temporary station at Mumps was closed, to be replaced by another one at Glodwick Road in November 1862, to which OA & GB trains now ran. Thus, the wildest dreams of the people of Oldham were realised, some might say exceeded by the provision of four new stations in a short space of time and within a limited area. Credit for this development must go in a large part to the MS & L who provided an excellent service of trains which has not been matched since; Manchester-Oldham in 20 minutes with one stop at Ardwick being the best example.

The next piece of the jigsaw to be inserted was the link between Oldham Mumps and Rochdale, a purely L & Y concern for which the company obtained an Act in 1859. This left Rochdale at the east end, a good idea in that it allowed the circular type of working as is met with today to and from Manchester Victoria, then the line turned south through the stations of Milnrow, New Hey, Shaw & Crompton and Royton Jc. The route reached its highest point at Hartford, before falling towards Oldham. In the Act was included a short branch to Royton on the west side, from the eponymous junction. Royton was close to the main line but, due to its rate of expansion, it was considered potentially lucrative and worthy of its own terminus. Trains ran on the branch for just over a century, from 21st March 1864 to 18th August 1966. A somewhat similar situation existed at Middleton where a branch line was put in, running north westwards from the junction and opened on 5th January 1857. This lasted until 7th September 1954, just before Middleton Jc. itself closed on 3rd January 1966.

At Stalybridge the old station of 1846 was closed after three years, becoming the obligatory goods depot for a new station jointly owned by the MS & L, L & Y and LNWR whose trains began to use it from August 1849. There appears to have been no ruling set down over the maintenance of the station, shared as it was among the three parties, so after more acrimony the L & Y reopened its old station for use in 1869 and inhabited it until 2nd April 1917.

Improvements took effect at Stalybridge from 21st May 1885 and at Guide Bridge around 1873.

Before moving elsewhere in the Manchester area to trace developments, it will be neater for reference purposes to outline the subsequent additions to routes in the Ashton-Stalybridge-Oldham areas. A key location was at

Denton on the Stockport (Heaton Norris)-Guide Bridge line of the LNWR. From Denton Jc. a line was opened which ran north to Crowthorne Jc. from 14th February 1876. This gave LNWR trains access to the OA & GB line and avoided the activities at Guide Bridge. Two months later LNW passenger trains were put on between Stockport and Oldham. A second line ran from Denton Jc. to Dukinfield, passing north beneath the Guide Bridge layouts and coming up parallel with the MS & L Stalybridge branch. This route, again, avoided operations at Guide Bridge and formed a direct LNW route to Stalybridge where it could connect directly with its own Leeds line, opened to goods 1st August 1893 and to passengers one week later. There were stations at Dukinfield and Ashton and Hooley Hill (closed between 1917 and 1921), both finally closing 25th September 1950. LNW passenger trains served Guide Bridge through the Hooley Hill station which was not far from the MS & L premises.

Denton Jc. had now acquired three routes, and the 'split' was governed by a tall and impressive junction bracket signal with posts of the same height. The LNWR still had one line to lay, however, and this was the short link between Denton and Droylsden, brought into use on 1st March 1882 and with one intermediate station at Audenshaw which closed in 1905. The line left the Crowthorne Jc. route out of sight at Denton Jc. from Ashton Moss Jc. and ran into Droylsden Jc. towards Manchester, giving Droylsden four platforms. The route gave the LNWR easy access to the yards in the vicinity of Miles Platting and a through passenger route between Manchester Victoria, Stockport, Crewe and Euston. An L & Y goods yard opened at Droylsden on 18th October 1881.

*A Class 5 enters Stalybridge from the west.*                    *H. C. Casserley*

*A push-pull train from Delph halts at Greenfield.*                    H. C. Casserley

Looking further ahead, in December 1885 a relief line was opened between Diggle and Stalybridge to cope with increased traffic on the heavily used double track which at times was sited on a rocky ledge up on the northern side of the valley. The new line pursued its own course at a lower level through stations at Staley and Millbrook (closed November 1909), Micklehurst (closed May 1907), Friezland and Upper Mill (both closed January 1917). The passenger service had begun in May 1886. Through passenger trains continued to use the line until closure in September 1964, after which a short section at the Stalybridge end survived to serve a power station. From Greenfield a branch opened in September 1851 ran north to Delph and was served for much of its life by the legendary Delph 'Donkey' rail motor and also by trains from Oldham extended from Greenfield, probably to avoid turning them round there. About half of them were extended in this way out of a total of 36. Clegg Street, Oldham had been rebuilt at the turn of the century to become the largest of the stations in the town, complete with island platform, bay and refreshment room. In May 1955 the service from here to Delph closed, the branch closing completely in 1963, while the Oldham-Greenfield section closed in April 1964. Trains between Stockport, Guide Bridge and Oldham finished in May 1959, when Clegg Street also closed to become a parcels depot.

To return now to the old M & L, later L & Y main line from Victoria to Rochdale. Blue Pitts station has been mentioned, and from here a branch of 1½ miles, opened on 15th April 1841 went westwards to Heywood, built without any apparent Parliamentary approval and worked by horses for the first six years until May 1847 when the first steam power was utilised. Blue

Pitts became Castleton on 1st November 1875. The company who built the line had their sights on Bury, four miles beyond, but Heywood was left as a terminus for several years until May 1848 when an extension was completed and the original branch doubled. The southern curve at Blue Pitts was put in to allow through running from Manchester. At Heywood a sharp curve marked the commencement of the extension, trains running through a new station there. There was one station at Broadfield and a timber viaduct over the river Roach near Bury. Some improvements took place on the line in 1883 and with the end-on connection to the Bolton line at Knowsley Street station, a grim looking pile, the route became an important one for L & Y services between Liverpool and Yorkshire avoiding Manchester.

On 17th May 1880 a new route was opened from Miles Platting to Werneth, relieving the line from Middleton Jc. up the gradients, though there was still a 1 in 44 over the last mile. Stations were at Dean Lane, Failsworth and Hollinwood.

The line from Miles Platting to Stalybridge, including the branch to Ardwick, resulted from the Ashton, Stalybridge and Liverpool Junction Railway Act of July 1844. The 6½ miles ran more or less due east and was to terminate in the same position as the SA & M branch from Guide Bridge at Stalybridge, with one long platform constructed alongside the other company's premises. John Hawkshaw replaced Gooch as civil engineer, as the latter was not enjoying the best of health. Work was put in hand by Messrs. Harding & Cropper on the line in April 1845, over dull and rather boggy terrain. There was a timber embankment at Park which was converted to embankment of more durable form in 1861. Another viaduct spanned the Medlock, with arches 10ft. by 30ft. at a height of 68ft. for 400ft. in length. Ashton Moss was a

*Ex L & YR 2-6-2T motor train at Holcombe Brook.*     *H. C. Casserley*

*Royton Jc., Royton branch on left, Rochdale line on right, Engine 51470.    R. M. Casserley*

bog and, at one point thereon a fairly deep cutting had to be provided, while the canal burrowed beneath the line at another. When it opened the line was single, though provision was made for a double track except on the viaduct which was widened on the north side in 1849 before the line was doubled in March. The structure was strengthened by steel struts in the 1880s when it was found to be groggy. The first trains ran to Ashton, a stone building with a roof of 150ft. by 60ft. covering the site, from 13th April 1846, reaching Stalybridge six months later. At the west end an improved station was opened at Miles Platting, straddling the junction with the L & Y main line. Stalybridge gained a big goods warehouse in 1884. The other, shorter branch ran southwards from Philips Park Jc. for 1 mile 1,561yd. to the SA & MR at Ardwick and was constructed by Messrs. Nowell, Hemingway and Pearson who found the task a slow one, consisting largely of low, curving viaduct, the arches of which were prone to collapse. The work took about three years, to 20th November 1848 to complete, and then things were only open to goods traffic. A passenger service began in 1852 and the line was doubled in August 1865. The line was, and still is, very useful for routing cross-city traffic, and exchanges were made at Miles Platting and Ardwick, where a station of sorts existed until 15th December 1902. An east-north curve was put in at Ardwick by the Midland, along with a line to their own Ancoats goods depot, while at Philips Park an east-south curve was similarly put in for use from 21st September 1890. At Beswick Jc. on the branch a short run of 26 chains went off north east to serve another goods yard and the Bradford colliery. This was opened on 6th March 1865.

The M & L extension from Miles Platting to Victoria station was opened on 1st January 1844 and the locomotive works were situated on land between that line and the run down to Oldham Road. The premises contained a five road 'straight' engine shed and a roundhouse with sixteen bays in it, both to the north of the main loco. and carriage shops. On the eastern side of the Oldham Road lines lay a further engine shed with eleven parallel roads terminating at the end of New Allen street. On 27th April 1873 a fire did great damage to the loco. shops and carriage works. The engine sheds were closed in 1876 when Newton Heath opened, while the works closed on the opening of the vast new works site at Horwich in 1888. Production of new carriages and wagons was transferred to a new works at Newton Heath on the west side of the line in 1877. Some tidying up of the site at Miles Platting took place, especially in connection with track improvements on the incline, though many of the old buildings were refurbished for use as stores and survived until 1967.

The old hoists for wagons at Oldham Road goods station were replaced by a 1 in 27 incline which was only built after St. George's church, which happened to be in the way, was rebuilt elsewhere in Oldham road in 1874. The incline came into use in 1877 and no doubt greatly expedited the transport of fruit and potatoes. These commodities were also helped by the widening of the approach viaduct and by the provision of a line across for it to the west side of the main line at Miles Platting into what became known as Brewery Sidings, the nearby signal box sporting the name and not too far from the Vitriol Works cabin further along! The L & Y was notorious for lavish signalling arrangements, and at Miles Platting were six new signal cabins

*The delicate rooflines of Manchester Exchange.*                    *H. C. Casserley*

scattered around, one of 92 levers, one of 50. A tightly curving east-north connection from the Stalybridge line round to Brewery Sidings completed the triangle at Miles Platting and was opened on 29th January 1906 as a handy link.

Oldham Road was a valuable property for many years and was added to, the most recent being new offices erected 1913-4 in the same style as Victoria station. All habitable structures went in 1968.

After the opening of the connection between the M & L and the L & M in May 1844 a link was put in at the west end of the Salford terminus so that Bolton trains could run through to Hunts Bank, though this they appeared reluctant to do; indeed, they stuck to their own terminus from 1849-52. However, reaction set in and eventually all eighteen of the Bolton trains used the Victoria station.

The new L & Y Company was formed on 9th July 1847 from the fusion of the Manchester and Bolton and M & L, while the LNWR, formed on 16th July 1846, included the L & M, Grand Junction, M & B and L & B. On 28th June 1861 the L & Y sought an Act to construct its own line alongside the LNWR at Salford, which was opened in August 1865 when Salford became a through station.

By 1853 Victoria was bursting at the seams, especially at the L & Y end where the gradient, plus a dark road overbridge and the Irk cramped the style

*Manchester Exchange, with a large invitation.*                    *H. C. Casserley*

of operation. The upshot was improved bridges and a suburban station adjacent to the main premises, known as Ducie Bridge and constructed of timber in 1855. To cater for the Bolton traffic the L & Y added on a couple of platforms on the north side adjacent to the workhouse. Opportunity was also taken to fit a new single span roof, supplied by Ardwick Ironworks. After ten more years further expansion took place on land acquired as a result of moving the Workhouse out to Crumpsall in 1876. A new iron roof appeared, completed in 1881 and a total of five through platforms were provided, with two cab approaches and extra bays on the Ducie Bridge side which date from November 1877. Electric lighting was tried experimentally for a time and the whole of the improvements were ready for use by May 1884. Extended office accommodation and parcels handling facilities were also provided; the L & Y handled a vast amount of parcels and newspapers daily. An electric overhead transporter, using 11½ in. gauge track ran over the platforms to move baskets of parcels wherever required. Operated by its airborne attendant it survived until the last war.

By 1904 Victoria had 17 platforms and its longest, No. 11 was linked to Exchange station which was built by the LNWR east of the Irwell river to free its traffic from the interruptions caused by rebuilding next door. It was a walk of one quarter of a mile before the long platform was officially finished in the 1920s. Exchange was opened on 1st June 1884 and passenger trains ran from 30th June. A Stockport-Victoria service was tried in 1882, dropped, then reintroduced ten years later.

In connection with the expansion of areas to the north of Manchester such as Cheetham Hill, Crumpsall and Whitefield the L & Y embarked on a policy of growth which included the improved route from Newton Heath to Oldham via Hollingwood and a new line to Radcliffe with a link to the Bury-Bolton line at Bradley Fold. These lines were authorised in 1872 and along with them was the loop which was to leave the Radcliffe line at Cheetham Hill and run to Thorpes Bridge on the west side of the incline up to Miles Platting which it would relieve. The loop line was a tricky construction with seven iron bridges carrying the four tracks. There was also a cut and cover tunnel of 262 yd. at Queen's Road. The line was opened on 1st August 1878. The Radcliffe line, which offered an alternative route to Bolton proved difficult to launch, as problems were encountered over acquiring land, especially through Lord Wilton's estate at Heaton Park, where a 713 yd. tunnel was insisted upon. A deep cutting at Whitefield caused problems due to the treacherous and waterlogged terrain. The line opened to Whitefield for goods on 1st August 1879, and to passengers on 1st December, the services running to Bury and via Bradley Fold to Bolton. Stations were at Crumpsall, Heaton Park, Prestwich, Whitefield, Radcliffe and Bury. A west-north link was put in to join the Bradley Fold and Bury branches at Radcliffe, making a triangular layout. Woodlands Road opened on 1st March 1913, Besses o' the Barn 1st February 1933 and Bowker Vale 26th September 1938. There was a rail motor service between Radcliffe and Bolton, for which a halt was opened at Ainsworth Road in January 1918. This was subsequently upgraded and existed until the line closed to passenger traffic in September 1953. The Bradley Fold to Radcliffe North and South Jcs. section closed completely on 2nd November 1964.

We now trace the Bolton line out from Manchester to Clifton Jc., opened in June 1847, from which point the East Lancashire Railway diverged on its course to Bury and Accrington. Accrington became a focal point of the company and from here lines led to Preston and Liverpool and, in the other direction, to Colne. This little empire was created in about three years, and the most important section was that from Manchester to Bury and Rossendale. Double track was envisaged from Clifton to Bury, and single line beyond. Hawkshaw was appointed as Engineer-in-chief, but due to heavy commitments on the M & L had to relinquish the post in favour of John Perring. The line left the Bolton line at Clifton in a westerly direction, passing immediately on to a 13 arch viaduct some 80ft. over the Irwell, a persistent river which caused the building of another viaduct near Radcliffe, a wooden one with stone piers at 70ft. in height. As often happened, the woodwork was replaced by iron, here in 1881. The same material was used for a 100ft. span just outside Bury. Bury station was an austere affair with a big, gaunt warehouse of a building on the east side housing the company offices. The line opened on 25th September 1846 and the first passenger train left Manchester Victoria at 12.35p.m. and reaching Bury over half an hour later. At Bury a further fifteen carriages were attached, and two engines brought the 600 passengers to Rawtenstall. Regular passenger services of 14 trains to Bury and 5 to Rawtenstall began three days later.

The ELR was dissolved in August 1859, though not before it had entered the railway history books due to its behaviour and its favouring of the Midland Railway, not surprising as it had an end-on junction with that company at Colne from the Skipton branch and could this work traffic between the West Riding and Lancashire.

It is obvious that the ELR and L & Y ran jointly to Salford from Clifton Jc., and from the outset ELR services missed out the Clifton Jc. stop. Then it was decided that they must halt there for ticket purposes from March 1849 and that they must terminate at Salford. Later on, pressure restored through running to Victoria from August 1853, but old habits die hard and even to the end some trains terminated at Salford. Much bickering produced a compromise and after they had considered an independent railway, the ELR reached an agreement with the L & Y whereby the Clifton Jc.-Salford section should be jointly worked as from 3rd July 1854. An extension of this was the practice of L & Y trains now running this way to Skipton from May 1876 via Bury and Colne. Trains to Accrington and Colne also ran via Clifton Jc. and Radcliffe. However, once it was decided to close this line nearly a century later on 5th December 1966, the services went via Bolton and Blackburn.

No history of the area would be complete without reference to the Battle of Clifton Jc.; thus the following is supplied for completeness:

Acrimony ensued when the L & YR demanded tolls from the ELR for using its section of line from Salford to Clifton Jc., especially as it was now possible for Midland services to run to Skipton by this route with the friendly co-operation of the ELR at the expense of the L & Y, as it were. The tolls would be raised legally under an Act of 1844 and were to be collected on site, a move which nettled the ELR who had hitherto been sending in returns of passengers carried to and from Manchester on a periodic basis. As from 12th March 1849 all ELR trains would have to stop at Clifton for ticket examination, to which the ELR objected, saying that up to then every payment had been properly made. However, the L & Y played rough and, after letting the first stopping trains pass without hindrance, placed a baulk of wood across the line to halt those due to go through the junction non-stop. The first of these was the 10.30a.m., and an empty train stood ready on the up line to take passengers forward to Manchester. The ELR train had no option but to stop, the L & Y requested tickets but were told that these had been collected at Ringley Road. Meanwhile ELR gangers removed the obstacle without trouble from the opposing faction who were probably daunted by a large police presence from Bury and Pendleton. The ELR train then drew up to the waiting L & Y train, following which the two engines engaged in a grand display of puissance to try to shift each other. Another L & Y engine came up from Manchester and the ELR blocked the down with a train of stones. By noon eight trains were halted in both directions. Eventually the L & Y officials withdrew, leaving an unfortunate passenger superintendent to mollify irate passengers after ordering the L & Y trains to withdraw.

Later that day things returned to normal. Until August 1853, however, all ELR trains terminated at Salford and some continued to do so for a century afterwards.


It will be remembered that Bury had been approached by an extension of the Heywood branch from the east in May 1848, when through running could be obtained to Knowsley Street from Manchester by using the south curve at Castleton. At Radcliffe, too, the railway map was enriched by the Manchester-Bury direct line and by the link off this line at Radcliffe to the Bury-Bolton line at Bradley Fold, all in 1879.

On the Manchester-Bolton Trinity Street line a station had been opened for a time at Oldfield Road, on the Bolton side of Salford station. This closed in December 1872. At Farnworth a new single line tunnel was supplied for the down line and the up was slewed to the centre of the original tunnel as from December 1880. This gave a lurch to trains leaving the tunnel at the Farnworth station end, due to the curvature of the track. It was, however, at Bolton that the most radical improvements were to be seen, demanded by growing traffic to Blackpool, Southport and along to Blackburn and Hellifield. The premises of 1838 had already been enlarged ten years after then, in May 1871, further alterations were completed. The down platform was extended beneath the road bridge round the curve to the Preston line, while the up platform was similarly extended back round the Blackburn line. New offices and public rooms were provided in a curved structure in Trinity Street. A long iron footbridge spanned Newport Street across the west end. In 1882 further platform extensions took place by 80 yd. at each side, while a new warehouse was provided in the goods yard east of the station. In spite of this attention, however, things were still unsatisfactory and operations were somewhat crude, especially the movement of goods trains at the west end which, if bound for points between Preston and Blackburn, had to be run into the station and run-round. What was lacking was a western spur to form a triangular junction of lines, and this was provided in March 1908 and gave much relief and encouraged excursion traffic between Blackpool and stations on the Blackburn line. A turntable was provided (unnecessarily) in the triangle itself and two new signal boxes complete with electro-pneumatic signalling were provided. New buildings were opened on the down side in April 1903 and the whole station was ready for use by February 1904. The layout was simple, with two long islands 71 ft. wide, booking office on the road bridge and clear runs through the centre lines. The whole station area was, and still is, most impressive. For a time from January 1882 the station witnessed the passage of MR Pullman sleepers on workings between

*The long platform linking Victoria with Exchange.*     H. C. Casserley

Manchester and Scotland via Hellifield. This operation had been made possible by the construction of the Ancoats curve which Midland trains could follow from Ashburys on to the L & Y line to Miles Platting, opened on 1st July 1889, and over which the MR could exercise running powers over the L & Y to Victoria and right through to Hellifield, some of the workings with MR locomotives which were outstationed at Newton Heath and Lower Darwen. As the MR had no 2nd Class facilities, L & Y six wheelers were attached beyond Manchester.

The L & M and the Bolton line were linked from February 1850 by a line running from Patricroft to Molyneux Jc. on the Clifton Jc.-Radcliffe section of the ELR. At Patricroft the junction faced towards Liverpool and the idea of the LNWR was to offer an outlet to Merseyside from the Bury area. This was not succesful and what passenger service there ever was ceased after three months without any intermediate stations to serve. Odd holiday trains used the route prior to 1939, and things came to an abrupt end in 1953 when a tunnel near Clifton Jc. collapsed and brought down a few houses in Swinton.

East of Patricroft, where a large LNWR shed was based, a line ran north west across the above unfortunate stretch of rails, opened in September 1864 to Worsley Jc. where was the division for the Wigan direction and Bolton Great Moor Street, a more direct route to Manchester than by changing at Kenyon Jc. The direct line to Bolton from Worsley was opened to passenger traffic from April 1875 with stations at Plodder Lane, Little Hulton and Walkden, where a high level station was opened by the L & Y in 1888 on its line to Swinton. Regular services into Great Moor Street ceased from 29th March 1954, though the station remained in use for summer seasonal holiday trains for a few years afterwards. Throughout their history the stations at Bolton remained independent of each other.

A line was put in from Tyldesley on the Worsley Jc. to Atherton line running south west through Leigh to Pennington on the Bolton-Kenyon Jc. line, opened in September 1864.

In order, now, to fill in the gaps in the railway network to the south east of Manchester, it is necessary to look at both Macclesfield and Buxton. Macclesfield, a silk manufacturing town of some 27,000 at the time when railways were all the rage, was one of those unfortunate places which missed being on a main line of route. Buxton was another. The first approach to Macclesfield was incidental, with a colliery branch from Cheadle on the M & B to Poynton which was opened on 9th June 1845, being extended to Macclesfield five months later. A station called Cheadle was provided at the junction, which became Cheadle Hulme after 1866. The North Staffs. Railway also ran trains to Macclesfield from Congleton, the line being opened in June 1849.

As noted above, the little branch of the MS & L to Hyde was opened in March 1858 and the logical thing was to extend it outwards, done by the Marple, New Mills & Hayfield Jc. line opened in August 1862, with stations at Woodley, Romiley and with a temporary station for Marple at Compstall.

*How the Miles Platting end of Manchester Victoria looked in 1959.    H. C. Casserley*

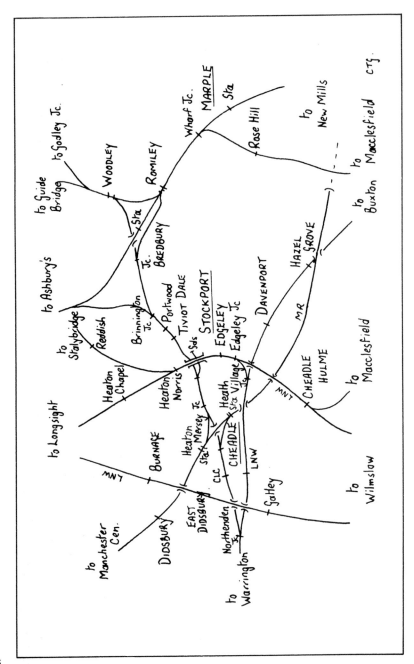

to Godley Jc.

to Guide Bridge

WOODLEY

Sta

ROMILEY

Wharf Jc.

MARPLE

Sta

Rose Hill

to New Mills

to Buxton  Macclesfield  Cfg.

to Ashbury's

BREDBURY

Jc.

to Stalybridge

Reddish

Brinnington Jc.

Portwood

TIVIOT DALE

STOCKPORT

EDGELEY

Edgeley Jc.

DAVENPORT

HAZEL GROVE

to Longsight

Heaton Chapel

Heaton Norris

Sds

Heath Sta Village Jc.

MR

CHEADLE HULME

MNT

to Macclesfield

to Wilmslow

to Manchester Cen.

MNT

LNW

BURNAGE

Heaton Mersey Jc.

CLC

CHEADLE

LNW

GATLEY

DIDSBURY

EAST DIDSBURY

Northenden Jc.

to Warrington

36

its line to Swinton. Regular services into Great Moor Street ceased from 29th March 1954, though the station remained in use for summer seasonal holiday trains for a few years afterwards. Throughout their history the stations at Bolton remained independent of each other.

A line was put in from Tyldesley on the Worsley Jc. to Atherton line running south west through Leigh to Pennington on the Bolton-Kenyon Jc. line, opened in September 1864.

In order, now, to fill in the gaps in the railway network to the south east of Manchester, it is necessary to look at both Macclesfield and Buxton. Macclesfield, a silk manufacturing town of some 27,000 at the time when railways were all the rage, was one of those unfortunate places which missed being on a main line of route. Buxton was another. The first approach to Macclesfield was incidental, with a colliery branch from Cheadle on the M & B to Poynton which was opened on 9th June 1845, being extended to Macclesfield five months later. A station called Cheadle was provided at the junction, which became Cheadle Hulme after 1866. The North Staffs. Railway also ran trains to Macclesfield from Congleton, the line being opened in June 1849.

As noted above, the little branch of the MS & L to Hyde was opened in March 1858 and the logical thing was to extend it outwards, done by the Marple, New Mills & Hayfield Jc. line opened in August 1862, with stations at Woodley, Romiley and with a temporary station for Marple at Compstall.

*How the Miles Platting end of Manchester Victoria looked in 1959.   H. C. Casserley*

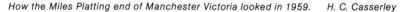

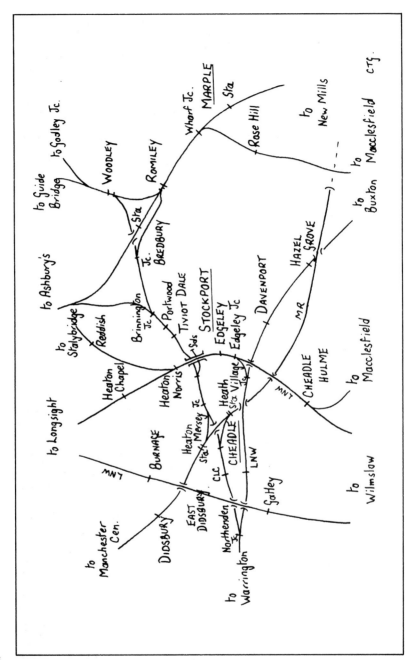

to Godley Jc.

to Guide Bridge

WOODLEY

ROMILEY

Wharf Jc.

MARPLE

Sta

Rose Hill

to New Mills

to Ashbury's

Sta

BREDBURY

Jc.

to Stalybridge

Reddish

Brinnington Jc.

Portwood

TIVIOT DALE

STOCKPORT

EDGELEY

Edgeley Jc

DAVENPORT

HAZEL GROVE

to Buxton Macclesfield CTg.

to Longsight

Heaton Chapel

Heaton Norris

Sds

Heath Sta Village Jc.

MR

CHEADLE HULME

to Macclesfield

MNT

to Manchester Cen.

LNW

MNT

BURNAGE

Heaton Mersey Jc

CLC

CHEADLE

LNW

Gatley

to Wilmslow

DIDSBURY

EAST DIDSBURY

Northenden Jc

to Warrington

36

From Marple Wharf a line, owned jointly by the MS & L and NSR, ran to a terminal station in Macclesfield, opened in August 1869. The line was extended to Central station from 1st July 1873 and stops were at Rose Hill, High Lane, Poynton and Bollington. The high level station at Middlewood was opened in June 1879 and closed, with Hibel Road station at Macclesfield, on 7th November 1960.

An extension from Marple to New Mills was opened on 1st July 1865, with the intermediate station of Strines opening a year later. The run of line was completed by the branch from New Mills to Hayfield, single and three miles long which was opened on 1st March 1868 and had one port of call at Birch Vale. From 24th June 1859 the whole route from Hyde Jc. to Hayfield was jointly administered by the Sheffield & Midland Joint Committee, the MR of course thereby securing for itself a through route from its own system into Lancashire.

The ways in which the Midland exerted itself in this direction make another interesting chapter.

*CLC Northenden Jc. near Cheadle, one of several very tall cabins in the area.   C. T. Goode*

*Skelton Jc, another tall CLC cabin, with the train standing on the Glazebrook line, the spur to Altrincham to the right and a line to the LNWR route to Warrington on the left.*
*C. T. Goode*

The Great Northern had an early hand in joint operation and shared working of the short Stockport & Woodley Junction Railway, opened in January 1863, with the MS & LR. Such lines have a habit of being extended to far horizons and this line, also joint, stretched to Broadheath where connection was made with the LNWR line to Liverpool, in February 1866. The route passed through Portwood (Stockport) and Deansgate Jc. near Altrincham. A fine new station was provided at Stockport, Tiviot Dale, with low arcades. There were also stations at Cheadle, Northenden and Baguley.

The LNWR ran a branch from Stockport Edgeley to Northenden which also had a station at Cheadle, closed in January 1917, from which trains ran for a time to London Road.

It will be noted that the jointly owned MS Jc. & A line ran north-south through Timperley, and where the Woodley-Broadheath line crossed it was possible to put down an east-north curve which lasted to 1903, by which MS & L trains could run circular service between London Road and the Central station, which looms large in the early history of the Cheshire Lines Committee and indeed of the MR in the Manchester area.

The impressive route between Derby and Manchester had the advantage of a good send-off via the North Midland line from the former city to Ambergate on its way to Sheffield, and it was to Ambergate that aspiring railway schemes were planned to run. One such, the sonorous Manchester, Buxton, Matlock & Midland Junction Railway, launched in November 1845 with a capital of £800,000 would start from a point south of Stockport Edgeley on the M & B to Hazel Grove and then follow the line of the later MR relief line to New Mills and Whaley Bridge, thereafter to Millers Dale, from which point the final MR route was to be followed. At the Edgeley end the proposed line of route was adopted by the Stockport, Disley & Whaley Bridge Railway, later the LNWR line to Buxton.

For the MBM & M Jc.R an Act was obtained in July 1846 and it was agreed that the M & B would supply £190,000 and the MR £285,000 of available capital; however the LNWR was formed on the same day that the Act appeared, the M & B disappeared and the scheme foundered. Next, the MBM & M Jc.R suggested a more southerly route which was more easily laid, to Hazel Grove, then a run south west of Buxton to Rowsley, all of this longer with no less than fifteen tunnels or 11,574 yd. underground! The trunk of this ambitious proposal survived in eleven miles between Ambergate and Rowsley.

On 1st July 1852 the MBM & M Jc.R became jointly owned by the LNWR and MR, uneasy companions, as it was obvious to the former that the MR was hellbent on getting to Manchester along their Hazel Grove route which was effectively scuppered when the LNWR opened its Stockport-Whaley Bridge

*Cheadle station on the CLC Stockport-Glazebrook line.*                    *C. T. Goode*

line on 17th August 1857, with stations at Middlewood, Disley and Furness Vale. The extension to Buxton was proposed in 1856 and opened on 15th June 1864. Seeing this, the MR suggested that they could run over the LNWR to Stockport, a ploy which the LNWR refused, though generously allowing local traffic to pass.

Meanwhile the MS & L were becoming agitated over LNW activity in the area of the Peak Forest Tramway, a line near to Dove Holes which it owned and over which, suitably improved, it might reach Buxton. At this period, then, we see the MS & L and MR united against the LNWR. The MR applied for, and

*Great activity at a former great station. Three services at Chinley, the 'Crab' to Nottingham, the nearest, a 2P, to Sheffield.*                    *W. A. Corkill*

won, consent for its Rowsley-Buxton section with a link with the LNWR at Whaley Bridge, hampered heavily by the combined opposition of the LNWR, GN and MS & L who had changed sides for a time. However, the mists of confusion cleared as two new Bills were passed, namely the Rowsley & Buxton Extension Railway of November 1861, and the MR & MS & L Joint Railway Act of 15th May 1860, which would now let the MR gleefully run over the Marple, New Mills & Hayfield Jc. line to London Road station. The Hyde branch had been extended to Marple via Woodley from 3rd August 1862 and on to New Mills from 1st July 1865, the whole run, including the Hayfield branch becoming Sheffield & Midland Joint from 1869.

The opening from the east to New Mills was delayed by a landslip at Buxworth which needed a new diversionary route on a timber viaduct. The first MR trains ran through to London Road from 1st February 1867. As from July 1871 the cumbersome initials MBM & M Jc.R melted away to become part of the Midland Railway.

And what of Buxton? The spa of 'blue waters' 1,000ft. above sea level found itself with two stations, the MR arriving on 30th May 1863 off a short branch from Blackwell, Millers Dale. Buxton was unique in that its two stations stood cheek by jowl with each other on the same site and, like Tweedledum and Tweedledee, of identical appearance, the owning company's name appearing round each semicircular window. The old route of the Cromford & High Peak Railway from Whaley Bridge to Parsley Hay was adapted to become part of the twenty mile Ashbourne branch of the LNWR which came in over the MR lines to reach its correct terminus and send a goods spur down in the Hazel Grove direction. Latterly a reverse curve linked the LNW and Midland lines, avoiding the termini, and using this facility diversions of Midland expresses did take place here when the latter company's route was out of action due to track repairs. In such cases an LNW pilotman would be taken on at Buxton and the working would run to London Road instead of Central. Until 1930 there were two locomotive depots here, but thereafter the MR was closed and the site used as a coal yard.

*'Jubilee' No. 45618 turns at Chinley.*                                    *W. A. Corkill*

The LNWR route to Buxton was spectacular with stiff climbs at 1 in 60 at Hazel Grove, Whaley Bridge and Dove Holes and a drop of 1 in 66 into Buxton. Almost 900 ft. was climbed in 17 miles. At Middlewood a connection was provided to the Macclesfield line. Some operating details are given in a later chapter.

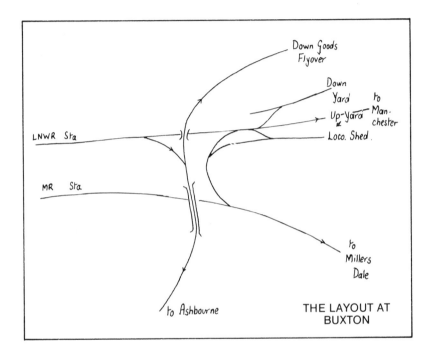

THE LAYOUT AT
BUXTON

The Midland, having gained access to Manchester in a manner reasonably satisfactory to themselves, now wished to strengthen their hand and were able to do so through the agency of the CLC, a concern managed jointly by the MS & L and the GNR, formed on 5th July 1865 and joined by the MR from 18th July 1866. The CLC was basically interested in linking Liverpool with Manchester, though their interests took them to Chester from Altrincham through Northwich and Knutsford. Initial portions of the scheme were the sections of route from Old Trafford to Cressington and from Glazebrook to Skelton Jc. (Altrincham), sanctioned by an Act of May 1865, plus the MS & L line from Godley Jc. to Woodley and the Stockport, Timperley & Altrincham Jc. Railway to Broadheath of February 1866. The CLC pushed on with their proposals and secured the running of goods traffic between Skelton Jc. and Cressington (Liverpool) from March 1873, and a passenger service from

Stockport Tiviot Dale to Liverpool Brunswick from the following August, to be run from London Road one month later over the line from Ashburys to Brinnington Jc, promoted by the MS & L in July 1866 with a branch from Reddish Jc. on that line to Romiley which, in actual fact, provided a cut-off route for the MR to London Road with which they were delighted. MR goods trains ran that way from 17th July 1875 and passengers from 2nd August, serving stations at Bredbury, Reddish and Belle Vue. An observer looking towards Manchester from the platform at Romiley would see a three way junction in front of him, with the Woodley line coming round from the right, the line to Reddish Jc. and Ashburys as the main route straight ahead and, off to the left, running parallel to the former but dropping into its tunnel the third line which was a shortish link round to the Stockport Tiviot Dale route at Bredbury Jc. This link saw passenger trains from 1st April 1875.

Meanwhile the CLC had obtained an Act for a new joint station at Manchester Central, to which the MR ran from 2nd August 1880 via Bredbury Jc., Stockport Tiviot Dale, Heaton Mersey, Chorlton and the delightfully named Throstle Nest South and East junctions.

To keep the growth of the Midland in one section, its later history will be included here. After aiming at Victoria station and the L & Y via the Ancoats curve, round which ran the through coaches to Bolton and Blackburn and the 'Scotch' Pullmans, and after the dallying with the MS & L to reach London

*Heaton Mersey in 1946. The station lay on the Midland route from Central to Stockport Twist Dale and the building was obviously in the GC style and similar to nearby Cheadle.*                                                    *Real Photographs*

Road, the Midland Railway had at last a station of its own in Manchester Central. However, the ultimate achievement lay in the Disley cut-off which ran direct from Buxworth Jc. to Heaton Mersey Station Jc., a fine route which was easily graded and saved 1½ miles, though this could be debated. There was first a 12 arch stone viaduct over the river Goyt, then a tunnel at Disley of 2 miles 346yd. Hereabouts the GC & NSR Joint line to Macclesfield crossed, while on a high embankment lay the site of Hazel Grove station, closed in January 1917, before the LNWR Buxton line was crossed. After threading a shallow cutting the line passed beneath the main LNW Crewe line south of Stockport almost at the point where the proposed original line to Ambergate was to leave. After this point matters became somewhat complicated with, first a spur off left to the CLC line to Glazebrook which was once used by MR expresses seeking Liverpool and avoiding Manchester. Then, after Cheadle Hulme the line crossed the Mersey and the CLC line to arrive at Heaton Mersey station, taking up a spur off the same CLC line from the Stockport direction. Heaton Mersey was regarded as the station 'for Stockport' and was opened on 1st July 1902. The MR then passed beneath the LNWR Styal Loop line which was opened on 1st May 1909 and ran from Wilmslow to Slade Lane Jc., and on to stations at Didsbury and Withington & West Didsbury. The line lost its identity at Chorlton Jc. where it made an end-on connection with the CLC, owned by them from 1886, towards Chorlton-cum-Hardy station and a rather dingy approach under tunnelettes beneath the MS Jc. & A to reach the triangular layout at Throstle Nest Jc., turning left on to the CLC if required or if running to Trafford Park sheds, or turning right to run

*A smart staff turnout at Withington on the MR line to Cheadle Heath.*   *Heyday Publishing*

parallel with the Altrincham line to join it at Cornbrook West Jc. The Altrincham line ran at a lower level on its own viaduct to Oxford Road station. The CLC approach to Manchester Central was on massive viaducts taking four tracks. The curved run-in to the station was made more exciting for the engineers by the need to cross some dockland and the South Junction line of August 1849 from Castlefield Jc. to Ordsall Lane, achieved by two substantial girder bridges with steel towers. Prominent to the left was the big GN goods warehouse at Deansgate.

There was a temporary building on the site of Manchester Central, opened on 9th July 1877 on what became the goods depot, and the CLC lost no time in running a fast hourly service of trains to Liverpool taking 45 minutes. The permanent structure was opened on 1st July 1880 with an impressive metal arch of 210 ft. in the style of St. Pancras with screen walls. The buildings at the business end were temporary timber affairs, as it was likely that something more substantial incorporating a hotel would materialise. This was not to be, however, the temporary became permanent and the Midland Hotel was to be found across the road to remind everyone of what could be achieved in the building line if one tried. MR trains ran to Cenral from August 1880, though some still appeared at London Road until 1884. From January 1880 a service of trains ran from Central to Tiviot Dale, calling at Chorlton, Withington, Didsbury and Heaton Mersey.

The Central station had nine platforms, Nos. 1-6 facing each other in pairs with an escape road between each pair making three tracks in all. No. 7 was an odd platform which started well down away from the barrier and projected beyond the rest, ideal for the spotter to watch comings and goings, but not for the passenger cutting things fine. Nos. 8 and 9, again, faced each other across three lines. There was a turntable off No. 9 which just fitted in at the departure side, while the 128 level signal cabin straddled the approach roads to Platforms 5, 6 and 7. Well outside the station was a double track junction to Deansgate Goods on the arrival side, where a ground frame was situated. Space was at such a premium here that there was little room to store coaching stock, except for a couple of sidings on the arrival side.

The MS & L was able to gain access to Central by means of a 7 mile loop from Fairfield to Chorlton Jc., opened from the latter station to Fallowfield in October 1891 and throughout from 2nd May 1892. At Chorlton the line trailed in to meet the Midland line from New Mills on the right. At Fairfield a triangular junction was provided and a new station east of the original one, and stations from that end were Hyde Road, Levenshulme ('South' added in 1952), Fallowfield and Alexandra Park, renamed Wilbraham Road in 1923.

At the east end the line was electrified to the loco. depot at Reddish and local services ceased from 7th July 1858. For a time trains such as the 4.35p.m. Manchester Cen.-Hull were steamed hauled round to Fairfield, where one of the electric engines took over. The GN brought its goods traffic to Manchester Central via Fallowfield and kept its own motive power there to shunt.
Midland local arrivals at Central included those off the Dore (Sheffield) and Chinley line, much enhanced in importance nowadays, opened for passengers on 13th April 1894 and with impressive tunnels at Totley and Cowburn.

From March 1967 all local Midland services were withdrawn from Central and such trains called at Matlock and Chinley only, and from January 1968 the remaining traffic went by the old Joint line through Belle Vue and

Ashburys to London Road (Piccadilly). In April of that year the Matlock route closed and all services went via Dore and Chinley instead. Chinley was a big station, opened in June 1902 and impressive with its sidings and pointwork. Faced with this, as well as the withdrawal of the Chorlton Jc. - Fairfield trains, the Central station was left only with its CLC Liverpool and Chester workings; the latter ran out over the old MS Jc. & A and beyond to Northwich. These could be routed at Cornbrook Jc. to Oxford Road and Piccadilly, and so Central was closed from 5th May 1969, a momentous day for Manchester as, at the same time, all Exchange station traffic moved to Victoria, except parcels.

The rather complicated network of lines in the Cheadle area was completed when the LNWR followed the example of the MR and built a new line bypassing Stockport to the west and running from Slade Lane Jc. near Levenshulme to Wilmslow, known eventually as the Styal line and opened to passengers in May 1909. Until the outbreak of war in 1939 some important Euston services ran this way, and a local service was tried, calling at stations at Mauldeth Road, East Didsbury, Gatley, Heald Green and Styal. Burnage opened on 1st July 1910. The area was not densely populated enough and the new line thus failed to drum up any new housing development. In readiness for what did not really happen, the six LNWR platforms at London Road were complemented by a small terminus of three platforms called Mayfield off the end of London Road, opened on 8th August 1910. Would-be passengers had to walk the length of the main station and pass over a long footbridge to reach their trains. Mayfield ultimately dealt with parcels only and was closed from 26th August 1960 after some suburban trains had been routed to Oxford Road.

To bring the London Road station area up to date; the whole site was remodelled as Piccadilly in 1959, when the South Junction platforms were made part of the package. From September 1958 Altrincham trains terminated at Oxford Road, allowing work to proceed on converting the short section to London Road to the same voltage as that on the Crewe line, off which suburban trains could now run, eventually through to Altrincham from 3rd May 1971.

To this day there is still a feeling of division in Piccadilly station as one arrives on, say, a Hadfield line electric and slips in alongside the more frenetic activity on the old LNWR side. Electrification of the Styal line was completed in 1959 with vast resignalling and upgrading work. Longsight station went on 15th September 1958 and Heaton Norris on 2nd March 1959.

The name Piccadilly became official from 12th September 1960.

The old Midland line from Central station via Cheadle to St. Pancras enjoyed a boom in express services for the period of electrification between Euston and Crewe between 1960 and 1966.


Years before the MR and LNWR improvements had taken place the L & Y had tidied up, some might well say, complicated its lines west of Manchester by laying a direct line, opened in June 1887 from Windsor Bridge, just outside Salford, to Swinton, then on to Atherton in July and Hindley in October 1888. There were stops at Moorside and Wardley, Walkden which became High Level in 1924 and Daisy Hill, opened on 1st June 1889. At

Dobbs Brow Jc. there was a connection with the Hindley-Blackrod line which offered an alternative route to Preston avoiding Bolton and cut down the Manchester-Liverpool route to 36 miles, the expresses matching the CLC's 45 minutes between the two cities. As a result of this new line, Pendleton received a second station at Broad Street.

The Sheffield, Ashton & Manchester Railway, later the Manchester, Sheffield & Lincolnshire, has still to have its early history more clearly traced. The company was incorporated on 5th May 1837 under Lord Wharncliffe and with a bevy of directors, including three Sidebottoms. The most interesting member of the heirarchy was, however, the Engineer, Charles Vignoles, who was an expert in his field. Meetings were not held exclusively in Manchester, but also at Sheffield and Stalybridge. The very first proposal was that of a line from a site in Store street, Manchester, through Gorton and Ashton with a short branch to Stalybridge, on to Hyde and Glossop and embrace a longer tunnel in order to secure maximum gradients of no more than 1 in 120. By an Act of 5th May 1837 the SA & MR was able to enjoy the run of ¾ miles over the M & B to the new Joint station at London Road, near to which was an office at No. 15 Piccadilly. Office premises were also to be found in Sheffield. From the beginning a desire was expressed to link up across Manchester with the L & Y and L & M, but nothin fruitful was achieved.

On 17th November 1841 the first train of five carriages left for Godley along the 8¼ mile stretch eastwards which included stations at Fairfield, Ashton & Hooley Hill (Guide Bridge), Dukinfield (Dog Lane), Newton & Hyde and Godley Toll Bar (station for Glossop). This was initially a single line, but double over the M & B section and a no smoking run at that, either on trains or at stations. There were feeder omnibus services from Guide Bridge to Ashton and Stalybridge and of course one out of Godley for Glossop, while private operators went over the top to Sheffield.

After a period during which there was a passing loop at Ashton, the line was doubled and opened successively to Broadbottom and Glossop (really Dinting) with six trains each way and four short workings to Newton & Hyde. These ran at even hours from Manchester and took 45 minutes to Glossop and five minutes less on the return trip. Ardwick station was opened in November 1841, while Gorton was not to appear until 23rd May 1881. In October 1844 a 1st Class coach ran away at Newton and found its way to Manchester, where it was diverted into a siding without mishap.

Mention has been made earlier of Store Street station, where there were arrival and departure platforms separated by six roads, three of which on the arrival side ran to a large turntable. Offices were shared with the M & B, with the SA & MR premises at the Sheffield end.

Glossop was linked to the main line on 9th June 1845, when its single line branch opened, facing towards Manchester at the junction. The little line was originally privately owned and belonged to the Duke of Norfolk, whose lion guarded the station premises. The SA & MR took over the line after a year. Ashton station became Guide Bridge from July 1845, while Broadbottom became Mottram and the old Glossop became Dinting, opened at the junction on 1st December 1847.

Hereabouts were some heavy bridges, the Etherow viaduct at Mottram of three laminated timber arches designed by Locke and built in nine months in 1842. The structure was 506 ft. long and 136ft. high. There was also the

Dinting Vale viaduct of five timber arches and eleven approach spans totalling 1,452 ft. in length and 125 ft. high. The woodwork did not last long and was replaced in 1859.

By 1860, with an average of almost 250 locomotive workings a day it was possible to justify four tracks between Ardwick Jc. and Manchester London Road, the MS & L (as the SA & M had become) keeping to the north side, much as nowadays, but with access across over the LNWR (former M & B) to the Altrincham line.

Ardwick station was improved by lengthening its platform, while Ashbury's, named after a local wagon builder, hence the apostrophe, and known for many years along with its 'for Belle Vue' suffix, appeared in 1855.

The MS & L had been content to leave the London traffic to the LNWR; indeed, in their position at London Road they could virtually do little else. However, the GNR began to show interest in running over the MS & L from Sheffield to Manchester via Retford, a handy station for connections, though these were not made too easy at first, to avoid rousing the LNWR. However, in 1857 a new through service was put on, completing the King's Cross-London Road run in 5 hours 20 mins., the same as the LNWR but over an extra 15 miles which was more hilly. There were two trains each way. The LNWR promptly accelerated to 4 hours 40 mins., but failed to keep time. Thwarted, the LNWR resorted to bullying tactics at London Road, staff terrorising passengers and MS & L employees there with reports of unfortunate booking clerks ejected from offices. By June 1858 equal rates for freight and passengers had been agreed upon and by Christmas normality had returned to the MS & L.

*Beneath the roof at Manchester Mayfield.* H. C. Casserley

There was a doubling of the Stalybridge line in January 1846 and a new station at Dog Lane. In May 1849 the L & Y met the MS & L at Stalybridge in a Joint station which had separate booking offices and junctions on the site of the former station. Three months later the LNWR made a connection at the east end and that company appeared at Guide Bridge from Stockport at the same time. Stalybridge had its first improvement in 1858, receiving its ultimate facelift, completed on 21st May 1885.

The activities of the MS & L, later GC, are chronicled in connecton with the other companies with whom it came into contact. In 1954 the line between Manchester, Wath and Sheffield was electrified at 1,500 volts dc and a regular interval local service was put on by new units between Manchester, Glossop and Hadfield. A new Woodhead tunnel of twin bores was opened on 3rd June 1954. In more recent times the line east of Hadfield has simply gone, leaving the original units to carry on until December 1984 when things were updated somewhat by the introduction of a different voltage and rolling stock.

The Manchester, South Junction & Altrincham line has always played a large part in the movement of commuters in the southern suburbs of Manchester, and from the first there were thirteen workings in each direction, including one express. By 1900 some five million passengers were being carried in 73 trains each way, while by 1931 the number had increased to seven million on 99 trains each way. Between 1878-9 some of them ran through to London Road, the rest linked by short workings. London Road was

*The LMS side of Manchester London Road.*                    *H. C. Casserley*

the chosen terminus to 1890, and the South Junction platforms had been improved in 1882. Facilities at London Road were one side platform and one island, of which the outer face was a terminal line which had a siding for Warrington trains alongside it. Both lines went to a turntable which, incidentally, was later transferred to Heaton Mersey. The site was linked to the main station by a footbridge and by 1929 things had become so busy that electric traction was seriously considered. In addition to the Altrincham line trains there were services out to Timperley Jc. and Warrington.

The LNER earmarked $900,000 for the convertion and Sir Nigel Gresley and the exotically named Lt. Col. Cortez-Leigh were responsible for affairs. The changeover was efficiently carried out between February 1929 and May 1931 with electricity at 1,500 volts dc taken from a 16 ft. high current wire sustained by gantries at 220 ft. intervals. The 28 track miles were fed by a generating station at Longford Bridge, converted from 11,000 volts ac. at Old Trafford and Timperley sub-stations.

Rolling stock delivered was 24 motor coaches and 22 trailers, originally meant to be in sets of nine, but actually in groups of six and three. A typical 3 set would comprise a motor coach, trailer and driving trailer, the whole assembly 185 ft. long and seating 226. A 6 car set would have a motor unit at each end. The livery was a bright green colour with plenty of teak in evidence.

Prior to the first day of running on 11th May 1931 there was a rehearsal on the previous Sunday when a complete weekday service was run for the sake of loads of ballast in sacks masquerading as passengers in the seats, all this as well as the normal Sunday service of steam trains. The running-in period took two weeks, a trying time for all, and on the first day there were heavy delays and two failures at Cornbrook.

With 3 car units maintaining the normal service there was a 20 minute headway at 10/30/50 minutes past each hour from London Road and at 0/20/40 minutes from Altrincham. Rush hours saw 6 cars in a train formation and the trains ran between 5.20a.m. (up) and 11.50p.m. (down). All but two of the eleven 6 car sets were based at Altrincham, with one at Oxford Road and one at Sale for rush hour use. On Sundays the headway was half-hourly until 20 minute intervals were resumed after lunch.

Fares were always competitive and stations well placed in communities. The old cricket ground station was reopened as Warwick Road, while new stations appeared at Dane Road and Navigation Road.

In with all the above went the sixteen trains each way between Manchester Central and Chester Northgate and five over the LNWR line from London Road to Warrington via Timperley Jc., with extensions to Liverpool.

Highlights of activity on the MS Jc & A can be summarised as follows:

Until the opening of Manchester Central the CLC ran from London Road to Liverpool Brunswick between 1873 and 1880, and for longer, from 1870 to 1914 that company ran to Altrincham and Stockport via Deansgate Jc. The LNWR operated two trains each way between Oxford Road and Crewe via Northwich and Sandbach between 1880 and 1931, while the rear coach of 'The Midday Scot' was brought this way from Crewe to London Road from 1900 to 1924, an interesting manoeuvre.

On the goods side there was a pickup working between Longsight and Altrincham and daily freights out to Warrington. Coal trains would find their way from Godley Jc. to the Chester line and limestone trains came from Tunstead to the ICI premises at Northwich. At least one working in the early hours went from London Road to Chester LNWR over the South Junction link to Ordsall Lane.

In steam days engines found at work were nearly all GC types on the one hand, and a more mixed bag of LNWR types, 2-6-2Ts, Class 5s and Compounds and L & Y 2-4-2Ts. on the other.

From 15th September 1958 Altrincham line service terminated at Oxford Road or Warwick Road while conversion work on the section to London Road took place.


On the Bury line from Manchester Victoria via Radcliffe the L & Y had experiments with an overhead electric system using high voltage. In 1912 the section from Cheetham Hill to Radcliffe was opened in an area which had developed very nicely due to the advent of the electric tram which had reached places like Whitefield by 1905, devouring potential rail passengers. Holcombe Brook was chosen as the site of experiments, using the first high voltage dc. traction in the world. The units used were two motor and two trailer coaches. The decision was made to electrify the Bury line in 1913, using the third rail system at 1,200 volts dc. Clifton Jc. was chosen as the site for the power station, not exactly adjacent to the lineside, but near to the canal. There was also a high rail embankment for tipping coal. Nearer to the scene of the action were the substations at Radcliffe and Manchester Victoria, to which power was conveyed by masts and copper wire. A feature of the scheme was the side contact pickup rail which could be boxed in because of the high voltage. Electric trains began running from 17th April 1916, in spite of wartime delays in supplying rolling stock from Horwich Works. The running time between Manchester and Bolton was reduced from 32 to 24 minutes, while there was a 70% increase in revenue in the first year. Of the 160 trains run daily, only 40 were well filled, however; the usual commuter story of morning and evening peaks. Trains comprised 5 car sets with seats for 72 First and 317 Third Class passengers. In 1917 Holcombe Brook was converted to the main system, and in 1931 Clifton Jc. power station was taken over by the Lancs. Electricity Board, to be closed in 1933 when power was taken from the grid.

Branch trains on the Holcombe Brook service were withdrawn in March 1951, after which what survived there was worked by steam. During the period 1959-60 the original L & Y coaches were replaced by BR Wolverton designs.

In the first year of electrification there were 57 trains booked to leave Manchester Victoria on the Bury line, including Saturday workings, with ten turning at Radcliffe and the others making connection at Bury for Ramsbottom and Bacup. In 1925 the offering was a 20 minute headway from 5.50a.m. to 11.30p.m. with a half-hourly service on Sundays from 7.50a.m. to 9.20p.m. There were several extras and short workings from each end, out to Prestwich and Radcliffe. By 1951 the service had reached 'frequent' pro-

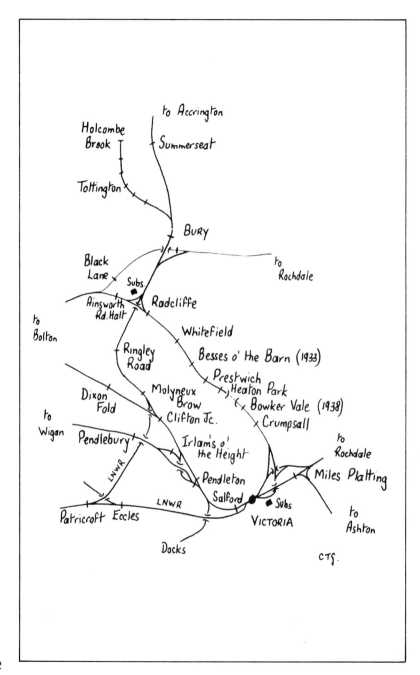

portions with trains every 5-10 minutes and a half-hourly service on Sundays. During the war in 1942 a steam train began the day at 5.15a.m from Victoria, followed by services to Bury at 10/25/50 past each hour to 11.10 p.m. Life began on Sundays at 6.55 a.m., followed by an hourly service from 7.50a.m. to 10.00p.m. and 11.00p.m. At the time of writing the service is at ten minute intervals during the morning and evening rush hours, then every 15 minutes during the day and every half hour after 6.00p.m. The run takes 23 minutes and there is, rather surprisingly, no Sunday service.

Of the other routes to Bury, that via Clifton Jc. formed part of a long, slow and interesting run to Colne and Skipton. In 1914 there were 30 down trains, including Saturdays Onlys, most running through to Colne and express to Bury Bolton Street. Eleven of these trains started from Salford. If Ringley Road station is taken as an example of what was on offer, then a total of eleven trains stopped there each way. In 1925 there were fourteen down trains with all but one halting at Ringley Road. Six started at Salford and most ran through to Colne, which was reached in 2 hours on a slow train. Some services to Accrington went via Blackburn and Bolton. In the reverse direction there were 16 up trains. By 1942 the number of down trains had dropped to 12, with 11 stops at Ringley Road. One train only originated at Salford and on Sundays there were four workings to Colne, plus one to Accrington only.

Things were still active in 1951 with 16 trains to Colne via Clifton Jc., two getting to Skipton. Thus the 2.5p.m. from Victoria arrived there at 4.20p.m. Ringley Road saw eight trains each way. On Sundays there were five trains

*Bury electric unit entering Manchester Victoria.*          *H. C. Casserley*

and of these, two reached Skipton. The third route to Bury went to Knowsley Street station via Miles Platting and Heywood, and in 1914 19 trains were to be found on this route, while there was a choice of four more services if the passenger went to Castleton and crossed to the other side. On Sundays there were six through trains. Improvements came in 1925 when there were 23 direct trains, most of them stopping at all stations and nine options via Castleton. In the up direction were 27 trains and 14 options via the Castleton change. This was a good service, particularly for the intermediate stations. The run took thirty minutes, though express runs were fast, as with the 9.30a.m. which arrived in Bury at 9.49 a.m. Things had cooled off by 1942 when only fifteen trains ran to Bury via Heywood, though eight ran through to Bacup.

There were three through trains on Sundays. The picture was largely similar in 1951, except that the three Sundays trains ran to Ramsbottom only.

The LNWR had a good road to Liverpool, flat and, it must be admitted, uninteresting. The progress of express trains was hampered en route by several stops,though fortunately no more than one or two these was served by any particular train. Even with a stop, the fastest run was made in 40 minutes and similar timings were achieved by the fifteen fastest trains in 1914. Thus the 12 noon train from Exchange reached Liverpool Lime Street at 12.40p.m. with a stop at St. Helen's, while the 1 p.m. took a similar 40 minutes, this time halting at Earlestown. Other services halted at Newton-le-Willows or Edge Hill. The longest time taken by an all-stations train was 1¾ hours, while certain slow trains went via Tyldesley and Kenyon Jc. One

*Bury Bolton St. terminus of the electrics. Interesting gymnastic signalling.    H. C. Casserley*

curiousity was a Mondays Only train at 5.55a.m. which went all stations to Edge Hill and then turned north to Stanley. In the reverse direction there were twenty expresses from Liverpool, with three non stoppers at 2 p.m., 5 p.m. and 6 p.m. in 40 minutes. On Sundays no expresses were run. Warrington was served by six trains on the Chester service which seems to have had departures at irregular intervals during the day. These left the Liverpool line at Earlestown.

Early post Grouping days in 1925 revealed a deterioration of services with only six or seven decent workings due to extra stops made at places such as Eccles, Patricroft and Glazebury, though there was one evening non-stop run to Liverpool, leaving Exchange at 8.20 p.m. and taking 40 minutes. In the opposite direction the 5 p.m. still ran non-stop and there were still more trains arriving in Manchester than leaving. Using the express service Warrington could be reached in 33 minutes, while late night Saturday revellers could leave Exchange at 10.45 p.m., pause at all stations via Tyldesley and reach Warrington at midnight. One strange thing about the Sunday service at this period is that the six stopping trains all went through Tyldesley in both directions.

One feature of the second War timetable was that seven expresses now featured as through services between Leeds, Hull or Newcastle and Liverpool. The non-stop days were now over and the best that could be offered was a 50 minute run by the Newcastle-Liverpool which left Exchange at 2.10 p.m. From Liverpool there were twelve fast workings, including three Leeds, two Newcastles and one Hull. On Sundays three cross Pennine trains reached Liverpool and only the 8.40 p.m. local running via Tyldesley.

By the time of the last period under review, 1951, the status quo had been restored somewhat with the 9 p.m. to Liverpool reeling off the miles in 49 mins. the best of an indifferent bunch of five fast trains. In the opposite direction there were still an unbalanced number of fast workings and the old 5 p.m. up had reappeared, making a praiseworthy effort of 47 mins. with three stops. Warrington was now much better served by a dozen decent workings, the 10.20 p.m. reaching there at 10.50 p.m. en route to Holyhead. The very useful 11.55 a.m. to North Wales via Warrington was now well established. The Tyldesley option still featured, with one train to Kenyon Jc. at 7.05 a.m. on Weekdays and an extra at 12.20 p.m. on Saturday. On Sundays five slow trains took this route to Liverpool.

Indifferent motive power, rolling stock and trackwork, plus more demanding movements at intermediate stations had caused some deterioration of the fine service which had been on offer before the Great War.

The L & Y had a different policy for its Liverpool services, which did not suffer from the imposition of intermediate stations. The 1914 timetable was a neat affair with 11 non-stop workings leaving at regular intervals and most taking 40 mins., as did the 10 a.m., 10.45 a.m., 11.40 a.m., then the 12.30 p.m. which took 45 mins. The 4.30 p.m. had a dining car. On Sundays there was one non-stop which left Victoria at 9.30 a.m. and took 45 minutes.

In 1925 there were still 11 non-stop runs which were all taking 45 mins., and the pattern of departures was now 9.30 a.m., 10.50 a.m., 11.50 a.m. and 12.30 p.m. while the 4.30 p.m. was as before, though five minutes slower.

The 1942 timetable produced a surprise, with all through trains to Liverpool Exchange terminating at Kirkdale and passengers changing to the local service. Even with this drawback the 9.35 a.m. service out of Victoria covered the run in 54 mins. The only train which ran through unscathed was the 9.40 p.m. (also on Sundays) getting to Exchange at 10.38 p.m. Times for the run in 1951 were 48 or 49 mins. and trains were advertised as through between Leeds, York, Newcastle or Rochdale. There were two expresses on Sundays, namely the 3.42 p.m. and the wartime train, now at 9.35 p.m.

Much of the traffic around Rochdale and the Oldham area was in the hands of the 2-6-4Ts in the last stages of steam power during the 1950s, when a few passenger trains still ran up the Werneth incline. This way was traversed by the 6.40 a.m. Middleton Jc.-Werneth and by three or four trains each way from Middleton Jc. to Rochdale and return. There was also a 3.17 a.m. MX Manchester Victoria-Rochdale-Bury Knowsley St. parcels which boxed the compass on its travels, a daily goods from Middleton Jc. to Chadderton and a freight at 8.50 p.m. from Oldham which went down the 1 in 27!

Bigger trains were often double-headed, as on one occasion in 1955 when two K3 2-6-0s brought a Skegness-Oldham working from Guide Bridge, after which one of the engines returned to Newton Heath via Rochdale with the empties.

From Rochdale the Bury-Bolton line was always regarded as a continuous route to Wigan, thence to Liverpool Exchange, Southport and Blackpool. Some interesting workings thereover were the 11.40 a.m. Rochdale-Hellifield, the 11.47 a.m. SO Bolton-Leeds, 9.05 a.m. Liverpool-Bolton-Scarborough and 11.20 a.m. return, summer Saturday workings at 6.09 a.m. and 12.02 p.m. from Manchester to Bolton Trinity Street via Castleton and the 8.37 p.m. Bolton-Leicester parcels via Oldham and the Hollingwood line. Prewar a train left Victoria on Fridays at 10.40 p.m. running all stations to Oldham, then Rochdale, Castleton, Bolton, Hellifield and Glasgow. In February 1953 for the Arsenal v. Burnley match 'Royal Scots' 46131/44/46 brought supporters via Stockport, Denton, Droylesden, the east curve at Miles Platting and Rochdale. Just as spectacular was the appearance of a Carlisle Upperby 'Scot' on the 9.15 a.m. Keswick-Victoria which, after unloading, took its empty train off platform 15 to Horwich carriage sidings via Bury.

There were some steam workings over electrified sections right to the end, as of course the Bury-Bacup workings and the 5.10 a.m. and 10 a.m. Manchester- Colne services which shared the lines as far as Radcliffe. For some operational reason in the 1950s the 3.12 p.m. Manchester-Oldham took the electrified lines out of Victoria, then went across to Cheetham Hill Jc.

A word here about slip coach workings which were to be found exclusively on the L & Y in the Manchester area. Slip coaches were especially popular on the Great Western out of Paddington and these were simply one or more vehicles at the tail end of a train which were detached at some speed and allowed to run, under the control of an extra guard, into a station en route. One of the last places served in this way by the GWR was Bicester. The disadvantage of the method, the risk of error, the problem of collecting up the coaches after use, the extra manning; all will be obvious, set against the saving of two or three minutes' running time. However Rochdale became an important 'slipping' point, with five Leeds-Manchester expresses each slipping two coaches there in 1889 and with Normanton and York services to Manchester carrying slips at various times. In 1901 there were six daily slips, while in 1915 there was still one slip off the 9.15 a.m. Leeds-Manchester. Sometime the coach would be transferred on arrival at Rochdale to a Southport train, as happened in 1904.

Not to be outdone, Accrington had slip 'arrivals' off the 4.25 p.m. Salford-Colne in 1914 on certain weekdays, running as a separate train at other times until the slip idea went in 1919. In 1915 the 3.25 p.m. Manchester-Colne slipped at Accrington until its re-routing via Blackburn in 1919. All ex L & Y slip workings vanished after about 1927.


The youngest participant in the race from Manchester to Liverpool, the CLC, was probably the most efficient, with a most impressive timetable, certainly on paper. To begin with, in 1914 there was a basic service of 42 local trains between Manchester and Glazebrook, including Saturdays Only, with fifteen of these to Irlam only. On Sundays there were 16 locals. In with these on up and down tracks were fitted 28 services to Liverpool Central,

*Flixton CLC station on that company's main line*  H. C. Casserley

nearly all express with one obligatory stop at Warrington. Basically the express left Manchester Central at half past each hour with extras on the hour, and the run was covered in 45 minutes. The return was made from Liverpool at half past the hour. On Sundays things were not so sparkling, with eight through trains and one express to Liverpool at 2 p.m.

Out of Central in 1942 twelve trains left for Chester and five for Northwich, these running express to Altrincham in order not to cramp the style of the MS Jc. & A services.

Throughout the periods under review the number of local trains to Glazebrook remained consistently steady at 42 on weekdays including Saturdays Onlys, though the through service fluctuated somewhat, with a wartime reduction to 16 trains to Liverpool in 1942, eight of them express workings, all taking 56 minutes with the Warrington stop. One service, the Hull-Liverpool which left Central at 1.46 p.m. managed to call almost everywhere en route. On Sundays there were five semi-fast trains at this time.

As often seems to have happened, by 1951 there was a livening up of things and the timetable showed 29 Manchester-Liverpool trains, half of these being express leaving a half past the hour and taking 52 minutes. There were two non-stop trains (how these got through Warrington without being challenged is a mystery!) the 10.05 a.m. down and the 2.42 p.m. Liverpool-Harwich boat train which took 42 minutes. On Sundays there were 12 semi-fast trains.

*G.C. "Director" No. 62653 "Sir Edward Fraser" at Glazebrook.*          *C. T. Goode*

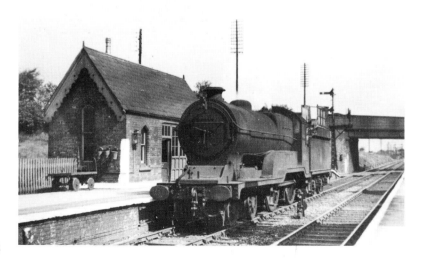

The CLC line from Stockport Tiviot Dale to Glazebrook was not well endowed with passenger trains, having but six or seven workings on weekdays only, the odd Sunday trains finishing after the Great War.

There was yet a fourth way of travelling between Manchester and Liverpool, which no-one actually pressed for time would actually use. This was the LNWR service from London Road via Broadheath, Warrington's two stations other than the CLC's and Widnes, definitely a run for the connoisseur or masochist which could take two hours. In 1914 there were seven such trains out to Liverpool and eleven back, plus four services to Chester each way and a similar number to Warrington Bank Quay. A train for Liverpool at about 10.50 p.m. which was most likely for mails ran into Manchester via Stockport and waited at Warrington BQ for 38 mins.

In 1925 there were again more trains from Liverpool (12) than to that city (8), non through to Chester but seven to Warrington BQ only. Sundays saw two Liverpool trains each way.

1942 saw a rationalised two trips each way between London Road and Liverpool, with six to Bank Quay and back. The late 10.40 p.m. ex Liverpool had also reappeared, booked to Leeds (arr. 1.52 a.m.) via Stockport and with a whole hour wait at Warrington.

In 1951 the above train was booked to York (arr. 3.37 a.m.) and there were three trains each way throughout and five Warrington workings. One curiosity was the 5.38 a.m. SX which started at Stretford and ran through all stations to Bank Quay.

As well as being a good performer on the services to Liverpool, the L & Y was able to cut a dash on runs to Southport and Blackpool, including club cars and refreshment facilities in the composition of the best trains to suit the well-heeled commuter, usually a mill owner. There were, in 1914, 25 runs on the L & Y to Southport, of which the 14 expresses took 48 minutes non-stop to St. Lukes, then Chapel Street (e.g. the 5 p.m. out of Victoria) and the rest up to 2 hours 3 mins. On Sundays there were two fasts and three slows. In 1925 the total number of trains had increased to 30, of which 19 were fast, the 5 p.m. now taking 51 mins. There was one Sunday and five slower trains. In wartime the total number of through trains had fallen back to 26, of which nine were slow and there were only four slow trains on Sundays. 1951 saw an increase to 34 through trains to Southport, with 21 expresses and the 5 p.m. now taking, as earlier, 51 mins. One express only was to be found in the Sunday service of seven trains.

Blackpool, being a more popular and plebean resort, enjoyed a more multifarious mix of trains and, as far as can be seen, even the fastest stopped somewhere en route. In 1925 one of the best was the 1 p.m. SO out of Victoria, arriving at Blackpool Talbot Road at 2.21 p.m. with stops at Chorley and Poulton, while the 4.55 p.m. ran non-stop to Poulton, arriving at Talbot Road at 6.06 p.m. SX. The LNWR made efforts to compete, using a change at Wigan; thus, in 1914 it was possible to leave Exchange at 9.10 a.m. and reach Talbot Road at 10.56 running via Eccles, Tyldesley and Wigan and halting at Preston and Poulton.

*Activity at London Road.* H. C. Casserley

In 1925 the equivalent service out of Exchange at 9.15 a.m. now needed 2¼ hours to Talbot Road with an obligatory change at Wigan.

In 1942 the 1 p.m. SO still ran and needed 1½ hours to reach Blackpool North, while the faithful 4.55 p.m. SX took an extra ten minutes. One feature of 1942 was the 10.25 a.m. from Exchange which called at Bolton, dividing at Preston into one portion which stopped everywhere and reached Blackpool Central at 12.17 p.m., while the other ran express to Poulton, gaining North at 11.57 a.m., an interesting piece of operating technique, though not unusual elsewhere.

The service still ran roughly to the same timings in 1951, while the conservative 1 p.m. SO (arr. 2.24) and 4.55 SX (arr. 6.09) still figured.

Nowadays the service is reliable but timings are not spectacular, due mainly to the desire to stop at places such as Chorley and Leyland. The 12.15 p.m. SO manages the run in 1 hr. 12 mins. with two stops, while the 10.46 a.m. non-stop takes 13 mins. longer!

The procession of trains leaving London Road was impressive, though still not as diverse as that seen at Victoria or Exchange, even with the London workings on the line to Euston, to which ten expresses ran in 1925, when named trains were the height of fashion. Thus, the 'Mancunian' left London Road at 9.45 a.m., into Euston at 1.15 p.m. and stopping at Wilmslow to take up through passengers off the connecting service out at 9.20 a.m. from Victoria used by those from Halifax, Huddersfield and the Rochdale. A similar service out of Victoria at 11.40 a.m. fed into the 'Lancastrian', out of London Road at 12.05 p.m. running via Stoke to reach Euston at 3.55 p.m. Several of the London expresses ran via Stoke, including the midnight sleeper which reached the capital at 5.40 a.m. On Sundays the same service ran, but without the sleeping cars.

There were other delights in 1925, including an 8.15 a.m. London Road-Aberystwyth (arr. 2.15 p.m.), a noon departure for Swansea (arr. 6.58 p.m.) and that celebrated pair the 'Pines Express' out at 10 a.m. and into Bournemouth West at 4.49 p.m. and the 'Sunny South Express' (lovely names these) departing at 10.40 a.m. and running through the Kensington side of London to reach Eastbourne at 5.52 p.m.

On Sundays the trains on offer were limited, with up trains to Euston at 12.30 and 4.20 p.m. and a Cardiff train at 10.45 a.m. Down arrival times on weekdays were 4.40 a.m. into London Road for the sleeper, 4.50 p.m. for the 'Pines Express' and 8.07 p.m. for the 'Mancunian' which left Euston rather early at 4 p.m. However, the 'Lancastrian' left town at 6.05 p.m. and gave a corresponding late return at 9.35 p.m.

*Heaton Chapel station on the LNWR line out to Stockport.*            *H. C. Casserley*

From London Road there were 22 local trains on the Styal line and approximately the same number via Stockport, turning round at Wilmslow or Alderley Edge, though 13 went through to Crewe.

In 1951 eight through expresses were booked to London Euston, with some fast workings to Birmingham and some via Stoke. The 'Mancunian' still left at 9.45 a.m. but took an extra five minutes on the run, while the 'Lancastrian' had lost its name but still ran anonymously to the same times and arrived a few minutes earlier! There was a Penzance train in the early hours, a Swansea at 9.20 a.m. and the 'Pines Express' out at 10.20 a.m. and into Bournemouth West at 5.32 p.m. The 'Sunny South Express' had, also disappeared into the sunset. The return working of the later 'Comet' from Euston left Manchester London Road 5.50 p.m. in the week and 20 minutes earlier on Saturdays only. The midnight sleeper still ran, conveying the supine to an arrival in the capital at 5.28 a.m. On Sundays this facility left a little earlier reaching Euston at 4.10 a.m. where, presumably, one could lie in until a reasonable hour. Sundays saw six expresses to Euston and a Cardiff/Plymouth service in the morning.

Stopping trains in 1951 were 23, with ten out of Mayfield station, from which some of the fast service departed. On the Styal line 17 ran nearly all as far as Wilmslow and a few to Alderley Edge. The practice was for Longsight station to be served only by Styal line trains. On Sundays there were five locals, two extended to Alderley Edge.

Both the LNWR and the GCR had interesting 'round the houses' workings in the eastern suburbs of Manchester, linking Oldham with Stockport in the case of the first named. Between Oldham and Stockport the LNWR ran ten trains in each direction in 1914, and two on Sundays, with the 8.52 a.m. In the reverse direction the 6.10 p.m. ex Euston conveyed a through carriage for Rochdale which left Stockport at 9.50 p.m. arr. 10.37. Other delights were a Stockport-Bradford working which left at 3.55 p.m. and a Huddersfield-Stockport which ran via Oldham Clegg Street which it left at 11.48 a.m.

In 1925 there were 14 services each way, with five on Sundays. The Euston-Rochdale through coach ran to approximately the same times. There were fast through services on this route from Stockport (5.22 p.m.) to Leeds and at 8.11 p.m. to Bradford with a through from Euston to Bradford this way on Sundays, leaving at 10.10 a.m. In 1942 there were 13 locals only from Oldham to Stockport and nine in the reverse direction, with one each way on Sundays. Nearly all the above workings missed Guide Bridge and passed beneath the junctions there at Hooley Hill. By 1951 the LNWR services had gone and the remaining locals, ten up and eight down went via Guide Bridge, with no trains on Sundays. A latterday development, though, was the running of trains from Greenfield at 7.40 a.m., 12.27 p.m., 4.20., 5.40. and 6.15 p.m. round through Oldham to Stockport, while only the 5.14 and 7.05 p.m. from Stockport were extended to Greenfield in the reverse direction.

Along part of the same route used above, between Heaton Norris and Denton Jc. trains ran to and from Stockport and Manchester Victoria via Droylsden Jc. Thus, in 1914 there was one local each way leaving Stockport at 8.17 a.m., actually running to Exchange at 8.54., and in the reverse direction at 7.47 a.m. Exchange to Stockport arr. 8.15 a.m. Four or five fast trains served Stockport and Manchester Victoria by this route, and some were through trains between Euston and Colne.

In 1925 the 12.10 p.m. SO and 5.36 p.m. SX ran from Stockport to Victoria as stopping trains, while the 6.48 a.m. went the other way. There were two Euston-Colne expresses and a through coach from Euston to Blackburn which left Stockport at 6.42 p.m. In 1941 the 12.10 p.m. and 5.35 p.m. locals and the 6.45 a.m. from Victoria ran as before. There was one through working to Colne via Victoria and two up services to Euston. A Stockport-Victoria ran at 7.57 a.m., also to be found running in 1951 along with the 12.20 SO to Colne, the 5.34 p.m. SX slow Stockport-Victoria, the 9.38 from Victoria (Colne-Euston) and 5.14 p.m. from Victoria (Colne-Stockport). Here was a good illustration of a blatant running-down process.

The Buxton branch enjoyed some beautiful scenery, severe weather in winter, hair-raising descents down the gradients with sad calamities, the worst of which, at Chapel en le Frith in February 1957 immortalised Driver Axon and No. 48188, one member of a rich assortment of motive power with 2-8-0s and LNWR 0-8-0s on the goods and pre-war activity by L & Y 4-6-4 tanks and LNWR 'Prince of Wales' types on passenger trains, while at the coaling stage an LNWR 'Chopper' No. 58092 or a North London tank would be on pushing duties. After the war 'Crabs' and Class 5s would be seen. Of the pre-1939 trains the best runners were the 4.45 p.m. and 5.50 p.m. up and the 8.18 a.m., 9 a.m. and 9.05 a.m. down services, made up of six coaches including two 1st Class saloons. The 5.50 p.m. ran non-stop to Buxton in 42 minutes, while the 8.18 a.m. to town ran downhill all the way in 40 mins. including a stop at Dove Holes! This was followed by the 9.05 a.m. with two stops in 57 mins.

Midland access to Buxton was chiefly by means of the shuttle service of trains to and from Millers Dale on the main line. There were 19 trips each way (12 on Sundays) in the 1950s and one through coach each way, that for St. Pancras which was collected by the 8.55 a.m. up train.

Considering the Midland approach to Manchester, perhaps the most worthy period to study here is that in early LMS days and between the wars. Prime workings included the 8.55 a.m. Hull-Liverpool, itself a 'foreign' train which split at Godley Jc., sending a portion to London Road while the main train went on to Stockport Tiviot Dale and Heaton Mersey, Throstle Nest Jc. and the CLC to Liverpool Central.

In the 1920s the 12.05 p.m. from St. Pancras divided at Derby, one portion running to Manchester Central via Cheadle Heath, the other to Manchester Victoria via Stockport, where reversal took place and the final run went into Manchester via Brinnington Jc., Reddish Jc. and the Ancoats Curve.

Up to 1939 the 9.05 a.m. Nottingham-Manchester conveyed a through coach for Victoria. Many of these workings were remarkably fast, the fastest being 3 hours 45 mins. between Manchester Central and St. Pancras. Before the Disley cut-off the run-in over LNWR metals was 4½ hours. Comparable times from Euston to Manchester were 4 hours 10 mins. to London Road and 4 hours 12 minutes to Victoria.

In 1914 there was one train each way which ran non-stop Leicester-Manchester and covered the run in 3 hours 40 mins. By 1960 there was only one remaining non-stop run, namely the 4.35 p.m. Manchester-Derby, when the 61½ miles were covered in 81 mins. In the same period there were four down and three up slows via Stockport, while the 7.45 p.m. Manchester-Derby ran non-stop to Cheadle Heath. From that station to Manchester Central there were four trains each way, and about the same number originating from Chinley. On the Hope Valley line there were two workings each way between Sheffield and Manchester, the 7.50 a.m. being non-stop from Chinley, reeling off the total run in 1 hour 34 mins., while in the reverse direction the 9.30 p.m. Manchester-Sheffield ran non-stop from Chinley. It is remarkable that this particular route had not been exploited before being 'discovered' on closure of the Peak route. Trains were never numerous between Manchester and Sheffield via Chinley. In 1925 there were but three out of Manchester Central, the 3 p.m. taking 1 hour 9 mins., with two on Sundays. These were supplemented by shorter local workings to and from Sheffield and Buxton, Chinley or Hope.

The goods workings, often forgotten, either ran as unit loads throughout or were reshuffled at Rowsley or Gowhole Sidings, then sent forward via New Mills and Reddish to Ancoats, to Liverpool via Cheadle Heath or Trafford Park via Disley.

*Heaton Mersey shed in 1952.*                                   *Real Photographs*

Already mentioned is the GN freight service from Codnor Park to New Mills via the Hope Valley line, though sometimes via Matlock. The principal service was the 8.22 p.m. from Deansgate to Kings Cross and the return which reached Deansgate at 4.13 a.m. Surprisingly, the runs lasted until 1953 and the GN depot next to the Central station, improved in 1898, closed in 1957.

The GN route was 13 miles shorter than that by the GCR through Sheffield. Kings Cross booking office favoured the GN route via Grantham and at the end of the 19th century the running time this way was 4¼ hours to Manchester, equal to what the LNWR offered. Through services by the GN to Manchester went after 1914, though the LNER did try their hand at a Kings Cross-Sheffield Pullman for a season in 1925.

The MR, like the GWR, was autonomous in its motive power, and normally only Derby types were seen up to 1935 when the Class 5s appeared. Trafford Park had many 4-4-0s of different vintages, and the first Compounds went there in 1909, while a batch of Nos. 1014-29 were on shed up to 1939. For local trains the maligned Deeley 'Flatiron' 0-6-4s were at Heaton Mersey, while Johnson 0-4-4Ts and LNWR 0-6-2Ts could be found on the Millers Dale push and pull. Freights were handled by the ubiquitous 8F and 4F types. Before the era of the 'Royal Scots', 'Jubilees' and later 'Britannias', of which six of the former class were at Kentish Town from October 1957, the 4-4-0s would either appear in tandem on heavy trains, or an older 2P would pilot a 4-6-0. With the advent of the diesels, including the 'Peak' class, things became easier and, dare it be said, more pleasant in many ways.

*A much younger author with friend at Trafford Park shed.*

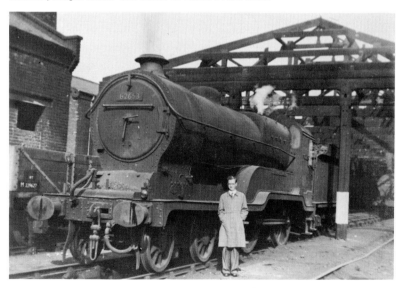

*These most interesting signals were to be found at the west end of Guide Bridge, where a Class K3 passes on a Cleethorpes express.* *H. C. Casserley*

The Manchester, Sheffield & Lincolnshire, later the Great Central, ran its independent way in and out of Manchester London Road station from the Sheffield direction, with occasional forays round to Central. The company's stud of locomotives was distinguished by its handsome lines and quiet efficiency, and the larger 4-6-0s could usually make a positive, determined get-away from a station without the histrionics of the LNWR products, some of which had been known to whip into reverse without warning. All this pageant could be watched from somewhere like Ashbury's station, distinguished by its apostrophe and well placed for the admirer to observe the coming and goings in the adjacent yards, on the main line, the junction off at the Manchester end striding out on its viaducts towards Miles Platting and that at the east curving sharply off to Belle Vue.

Actually, there was not a great deal of GC traffic out of London Road compared with the wonderful activity at, say, Victoria. Through expresses to Marylebone in 1914 numbered four, calling at Guide Bridge and Penistone, three to Cleethorpes or Lincoln and one, the 9.13 a.m. to Hull. There were nine or ten locals out to Hadfield, bolstered up by other stopping trains extended to Sheffield or Penistone. The 11.10 a.m. ran through to Glossop. On Sundays there were six workings to Sheffield, including the 4.55 p.m. to

Marylebone, two extended to Nottingham and the interesting 12.35 p.m. which ran to Hull via Doncaster and Selby. No services went into Lincolnshire. Additional to the above, in 1914 the observer at Ashbury's would have had many up and down trains stopping there, with a breakdown of the up trains as follows: (including Saturday Onlys)

35 for the New Mills and Hayfield line, of which 12 went via Belle Vue and Reddish and the rest by way of Guide Bridge. Of these, seven ran to New Mills only and eleven terminated at Marple.

10 for Macclesfield Central, of which three went via Belle Vue and Reddish.

12 for Stockport Tiviot Dale, nine running by Belle Vue and Reddish.

One could also change at Woodley for Stockport. On Sundays there were four Hayfield trains each way, four to Macclesfield and three to Tiviot Dale, all via Guide Bridge. As always, the oddities make the most interesting reading. as the 5.40 a.m. Macclesfield-Bollington and 6.15 a.m., probably a warming-up turn for the 'Bollington Bug', and the 4.22 p.m. Bredbury to New Mills, arriving there at 4.37 p.m.

Corresponding early second World War services in this direction were:

41 trains for Hayfield, of which 17 went via Belle Vue and Reddish. 13 terminated at Marple and only two at New Mills.

*Local service passing Ashbury's for Belle Vue.*                     *H. C. Casserley*

Macclesfield Central trains numbered 15, of which eight took the Belle Vue route. On Sundays the pattern of trains was five out to Hayfield, one to New Mills and five for Macclesfield, but only three trains returning on each route-old timetables often played this sort of trick and left one wondering if there was a pile-up of excess rolling stock at one end! All went via Guide Bridge except the 9.50 a.m. to Macclesfield. By this time the London Road-Stockport Tiviot Dale service had gone and trains were developed along the MR(LMS) axis through Stockport between Chinley and Manchester Central, with Marple and New Mills as important connecting points for the Joint Line through Belle Vue. Marple was well served in 1914, with five or six London St. Pancras trains calling there. The up 4.29 p.m. at Marple also halted at Bredbury. A total of 18 up weekday MR trains called at Marple, most being Manchester Central-Chinley locals, though some originated at Stockport Tiviot Dale. In 1914 there were only a couple of expresses evident on this line, but policy must have changed in early LMS days, as the 1925 timetable shows 13 Chinley-Manchester Central locals (including four Marple-Stockports) on weekdays. Curiousities included the 7.58 a.m. which started at Marple for Altrincham via Stockport, with two Altrincham-Marple trains on Saturdays arriving at 1.16 p.m. and 10.52 p.m. respectively. The Manchester-Tilbury boat train left Manchester Central at 5.50 p.m. and ran through non-stop to Derby, arr. 7.17 p.m., while the return working paused at Chinley at 12.27 p.m. to arrive at Manchester Central at 12.53 p.m.

By 1942 an important change had taken place in that the LMS service had settled to nine trains each way on a Manchester Central-New Mills service, with one slow each way to and from Derby and one to Buxton.

*Mottram & Broadbottom station on the GC main route to Woodhead.   Heyday Publishing*

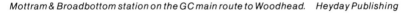

In the diesel unit era New Mills has become the terminus of local workings and the link-up station for Sheffield line services along the Hope valley. Units awaiting reversal can hide away in the tunnel off the platforms on part of the closed Hayfield branch.

The suburban line running through the south of Manchester from Central to Fairfield Jc. on the GC route out to Woodhead never quite made the grade, though the stations were solid and impressive and the trains adequate for a time. It was always an adventure to go and seek out a Hull train from the 'wrong' station at Central, to let the engine, perhaps a B17, pick its way past sooty signal boxes with odd names like Throstle Nest Jc. and slowly through Wilbraham Road and similar until, eventually, the main line was joined at Fairfield, made more important after the Woodhead electrification, as this was the place where steam was exchanged. A look at the timetable for the line gives a classic example of decline, and departures at Fallowfield are given as instances for the comparative years. Alexandra Park, later Wilbraham Road, did not open on Sundays.

*Fallowfield GC station.* *Heyday Publishing*

*An ex GC class N5 gets a lift at Trafford Park.* C. T. Goode

Departures from Fallowfield to Manchester Central. Weekdays 1914.
* denotes train passing through.

6.51 a.m. 7.38 8.01 8.25 8.55 10.08 11.00* 12.08 p.m.* 12.48 SO 2.05 3.55 5.35 6.14 SX 6.54 7.11* 8.11 9.02* 10.44.

Sundays
3.14 a.m.* 10.16 1.00 p.m. 1.19 2.16 3.50 5.30 7.36 9.24 10.40

Departures from Fallowfield to Fairfield 1914        Weekdays
7.23 a.m. 7.56 8.36 9.35 10.59 SX 11.39* 12.17 p.m. 1.22 1.40 4.44 5.52 6.25 SX 6.52 7.34 (takes up only) 8.39 11.01 SX 11.23 SO.

Sundays
9.38 a.m. 11.43 12.18 p.m. (London only) 1.38 2.53 4.38 6.23 8.28 10.43.

Departures from Fallowfield to Manchester Central.1914     Weekdays.
7.48 a.m. 9.00 12.45 p.m. 1.01* 4.15* 6.16

Sundays
1.01 p.m.* 7.56*

Departures from Fallowfield for Fairfield 1914        Weekdays
7.57 a.m. 12.18 p.m. SO 1.42 SO 3.44* 4.42 SX 5.41 5.57 SX

Sundays
10.39 a.m.* 5.39 p.m.*

Departures from Fallowfield for Manchester Central. 1951    Weekdays
7.48 a.m. 8.58 10.05* 12.37 p.m.* 6.19 SX 7.56*

Sundays
1.00 p.m.* 7.50 p.m.*

Departures from Fallowfield for Fairfield 1951        Weekdays
7.50 a.m. 10.50* 12.18 p.m. SO 4.29 SX 5.50* 5.57 SX 10.50*

Sundays
10.50 a.m.* 5.45 p.m.*


The area around Manchester has retained most of its rail links, with notable exceptions such as the Bolton-Rochdale, while some such as the Stalybridge-Stockport have, quite surprisingly, survived, even if reduced to the ranks of single track. Guide Bridge was just too interesting to last in its complete form and through traffic now passes on the north side away from the main building and the old yard and stabling point.

There are two strategies for the revamping of the rail transport network around Manchester, as well as some pretty little bouts of face-lifting for stations. There are six newly opened stations, at Humphrey Park (near Urmston), Mills Hill and Flowery Field, with Smithy Bridge, Ryder Brow and Derker. At the time of writing, six further stations are scheduled, at Lostock Jc., Crompton Way, Gatley Hill, Abraham Moss Centre, Smedley Lane and Godley, Mottram Road.

The most important project, certainly for long distance passengers who for many years have had to toil between the two major termini in Manchester, is the construction of 750 yd. of new line between Ordsall Lane near by Piccadilly to Windsor Bridge near Salford, which would be part of the eventual electrification between Manchester and Preston via Bolton, leading to the diversion of some of the express services between London and Glasgow through Manchester and Bolton instead of Wigan. Bolton was particularly pleased to hear the news of the decision, as a direct link with the capital will now be secured.

A more immediate improvement was the laying of a new link at Hazel Grove, costing £1.4 million, between the Stockport-Buxton line and the Midland cut-off route from Heaton Mersey to New Mills. The link is due to open in March 1986 and will provide a smoother run-in and out of Piccadilly via Stockport for services using the New Mills and Chinley route.

Addition to the above new stations, some of the old breed will be having name changes; thus Newton Heath (old Dean Lane), New Moston (Old Moston), Ladybarn (Mauldeth Road), Fog Lane (Burnage), Trafford Bar (Old Trafford), Salford Central (Salford) and a new station to appear on the Windsor Link to be called Salford Crescent.

On 9th December 1984 the Manchester-Glossop-Hadfield line was converted from 1,500 v.dc to 25 kv.ac., and the veteran 506 type units were withdrawn, to be replaced initially by eight 303 type units. The riding was just as rough and upholstery no improvement, though more daylight came through the windows which were not so cluttered by the door opening gear. The Glossop line is one of those scheduled to be part of a £95 million network lines on which light tramway vehicles could run in the same manner as on Tyneside, sixty miles of it in all. The first phase, costing £40 million, would embrace the Bury and Altrincham lines, linked through the city centre via Piccadilly, Victoria and Deansgate stations, Piccadilly Gardens and Market Street at surface level. The other sections of line, including that out to Glossop and Hadfield, would embrace Oldham-Rochdale, Marple and Rose Hill and a reopened section to East Didsbury. Adoption of the system would, it was felt, prevent the inevitable closure of some of the lines involved within a short period of time.

Electric coverage to Hazel Grove was completed by 1981, giving through services between there and Altrincham, where an interchange with road services had been opened in 1976. A similar arrangement was initiated at Bury in 1980, leaving the older stations abandoned in favour of a smart, new site. On the Bury line the newer units transferred there had been built in 1959 for the Crewe services, and the difficulties of operating the line with the original side contact rail, which was hard to service, and the half-century old mercury arc bulb rectifiers soon became apparent.

Other electric stock new to the area came from earlier Glasgow electrification. The reader is advised to visit stretches of line in which he is interested, in order to keep up with the latest developments, an often rewarding task. Currently the lightweight Leyland railbuses, worth a ride in if only to sample the interesting undulations on two axles, look very smart in the orange and brown Selnec livery as they cope with the gradient out of Victoria en route to Oldham and Rochdale. Victoria is in the throes of heavy rebuilding at the terminal end.

Along with the operating improvements must of course go signalling alterations, and at the time of writing there is a medley of sophisticated modern gear at work alongside some basic lever-pulling at Miles Platting and places out to Stalybridge, though every so often the odd mechanical signal arm will disappear, legally of course. Bolton West, the first power box in the country, is due to go under a £32 million electrification scheme. East box is a hefty specimen as well.

Stockport gained its colour lights as early as March 1955 when No.2 box and a refurbished Heaton Norris took on all the signalling up to Levenshulme. Heaton Norris, with 125 levers, still worked its points mechanically, while No. 2 was reduced to 45 levers. The scheme at Victoria East was due for the same year, but delayed because of cash shortage. Here six mechanical cabins were replaced by one control panel using thumb switches to set up routes.

London Road had an early power box scheme of 1909, with the GC side electro-pneumatic and the LNW all-electric, both retaining the original semaphores for a time. There were three signal boxes straddling the lines, with the two LNW structures gaining wartime concrete umbrellas. The new powerbox of 1960 replaced 13 signal boxes with a total of 848 levers by a console housing 491 route switches and 121 individual point switches.

*Electric locos. Nos. 26039 & 27001 entering Guide Bridge.*  *H. C. Casserley*

There were four stages in the commissioning of the new scheme:

1.   November 1958. Change in direction of running, Slade Lane-London Road.
2.   Alteration of approach lines, Slade Lane and Ardwick. December 1959.
3.   LNER side brought into use, April 1960.
4.   Remainder in use, August 1960.

Before closing this all-too sketchy account of the life of Manchester's railways, mention should certainly be made of the Manchester Ship Canal Railway, an influential and significant part of the railway scene which existed on the west side of the city and along towards the mouth of the Mersey. As with much of the material to be found in this little book, particular topics have been ably covered by more knowledgeable authors in separate works. Here in the limited space available, the reader must be content with an overall survey.

The Ship Canal was opened by Queen Victoria on 21st May 1894 and was basically intended to bring raw materials and foodstuffs and to send out manufactured products. The Canal Railway was established by an Act of January 1894 to run from Manchester to Ellesmere Port, stopping short of the Canal which went on further to the Mersey. The line traversed 33 miles of

'Director' No 62651 passing Trafford Park on a Liverpool Central Train.     H. C. Casserley

route and owned over 200 miles of track. It had at one time 74 engines, latterly 69 and 2,500 wagons, in which up to seven million tons of traffic were shipped at peak periods in its history, though wartime loadings would exceed this. Rolling stock was in grey, lettered MSC, while locomotives were in dark green with brass numberplates backed in red. There was also three coaches for use when needed.

Pomona Docks were closest to Manchester. Nos. 1-4 were on the south side at the start of the line. From here it ran for 2-3 miles along Trafford Wharf to the border of the Dock Estate and that at Trafford Park, where an Esso installation was situated. Trafford Park was once a beauty spot, the home of Sir Humphrey de Trafford of Trafford Hall. However, the prospects from his windows grew worse and worse, so he upped sticks and the site became an estate of 1,200 acres with some 200 industrial units, most with private sidings. Actually the Trafford Park Estate had its own rail system with outlets to the MSCR at simply named A and B junctions. The line had no rolling stock but was served by the larger company.

South of Trafford Park was the Barton Dock Estate, separated from it by the Bridgewater Canal. From here traffic was worked by the CLC at one side and by the MSCR at the other over the Trafford Park Estate line as far as a swing bridge over the Canal at Trafford Wharf. The swing bridge was fully equipped with the necessary gadgets to ensure safety.

On the north side of the swing bridge was the principal dock area, with Docks Nos. 6-8 and the largest, No.9, all equipped with open standage areas.

From the Irwell Park Wharf (Eccles) the single main line ran off westwards through Partington as far as Latchford. En route it passed beneath the Barton aqueduct which took the Bridgewater canal over the Manchester Ship canal, itself adjacent to a road swing bridge.

The Co-operative Wholesale Society had their Margarine and Soap works hereabouts, near Irlam, and had an outlet to the CLC at Irlam Jc., moving their own traffic with their own engines over MSCR track. Thereover, along with the margarine, went trains of steel slag operated by the Lancashire Steel Corporation from Partington to Rixton tip, about four miles over the single track.

The LNWR Lymm line crossed the canal and the MSCR at Latchford Dock by a 75 ft. high bridge, then curved and ran along the canal to exchange sidings at Latchford. Here the MSCR was laid on the formation of the old LNWR, formerly the Altrincham & Warrington Railway and passed between the old Latchford station buildings. The canal has a link through to the Mersey and the run of the MSCR is, for this book, conveniently broken here.

The line was controlled from Partington North and functioned by telephone communication, with permission to proceed given by messages which were repeated by the drivers. Signalling was minimum headway of ten minutes between each in fair weather. The chief offices were in Manchester, while a superintendent manned the Ellesmere Port end of things. There were 500 staff, including 110 footplate men. Connections with the main line were at Bridgewater CLC, New Barns L & Y, Weaste LNW, Irlam, Partington, Glazebrook CLC and Latchford LNW. The New Barns connection ran from Windsor Bridge No.2 cabin down at 1 in 47 through sundry tunnels and bridges. Traffic for east of the Pennines was routed westwards via Bolton and thence to Rochdale to obviate reversal. All private sidings, and there were 133 of these, on the Trafford Park estate alone, were entitled to two visits a day. Engine sheds at the Manchester end were at Weaste Mode Wheel Road (the biggest with servicing facilities and 30 engines), No.9 Dock, New Barns Jc., Partington North and South side, and at Warrington.

Below is the table of locomotives available to the MSCR towards the end of its existence.

| | |
|---|---|
| 26 | Hudswell Clarke 0-6-0s with short.tanks. |
| 20 | Hudswell Clarke 0-6-0s with long tanks and outside cylinders. |
| 8 | Hunslet 0-6-0s with short tanks. |
| 6 | Kitson 0-6-0s with long tanks. |
| 3 | Hudswell-Clarke 0-6-0s, Heavy saddle tanks with outside cylinders. |
| 3 | Ex WD 0-6-0 Saddle tanks. |
| 1 | Hunslet 0-6-0, Saddle tank. |
| 1 | Peckett 0-4-0, Saddle tank with outside cylinders. |
| 1 | Hudswell Clarke 0-6-0, Lighter weight saddle tank. |

Today Trafford Park is still the biggest manufacturing estate in Great Britain, though the workforce has dropped from 100,000 to 20,000, its most glamorous time being perhaps during the second world war when Lancaster bombers were built there. One quarter of the estate is now vacant, and the railway which would move any commodity at 6d. per ton for anyone, is now an eyesore. A new Trafford Park development unit has been active in restoring life to the area and has created 1,300 new jobs in four years. The area is due to be smartened up with the present lake converted into an animal sanctuary, the opening of museums and leisure facilities, at the same time pulling down old buildings.

Thus the new Trafford Park will depend not on the railway but on the excellent motorway links nearby which are readily available. The first of the £10 million invested will come mainly from county and government grants, and only ten per cent from the ratepayers.

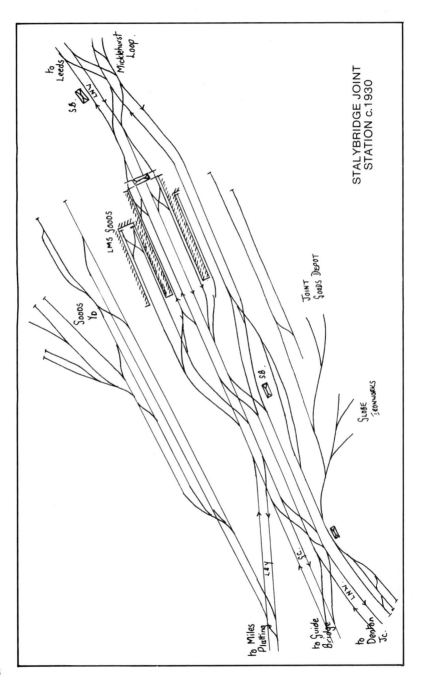

STALYBRIDGE JOINT
STATION C.1930

to Leeds

Micklehurst Loop.

S.B.

LNW

LMS Goods

Goods Yd

Joint Goods Depot

S.B.

Globe Ironworks

L&Y

S.C.

LNW

to Miles Platting

to Guide Bridge

to Denton Jc.

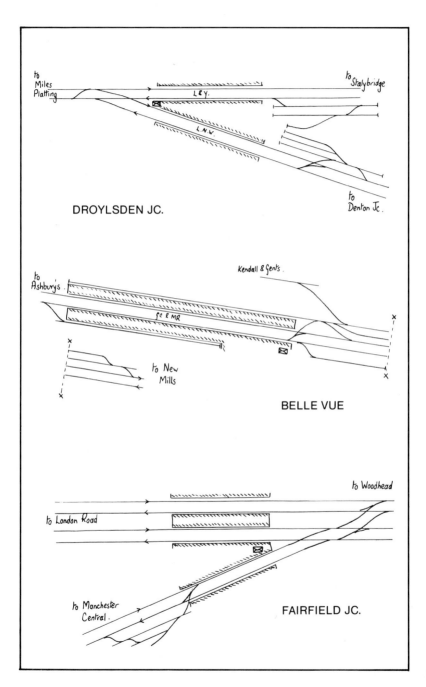

to
Miles
Platting

L & Y.

to Stalybridge

L.N.W.

to
Denton Jc.

DROYLSDEN JC.

to
Ashbury's

Kendall & Gent's.

S C & M.R.

to New
Mills

BELLE VUE

to Woodhead

to London Road

to Manchester
Central.

FAIRFIELD JC.

# ——FOOTBALL——

## MANCHESTER CITY v. DERBY COUNTY

AT MAINE ROAD                                          KICK-OFF 2.15 p.m.

## SATURDAY, 5th JANUARY, 1952

### HALF-DAY EXCURSION TICKETS TO

# MANCHESTER
### (CENTRAL)

| FROM | | | | TIMES OF DEPARTURE | RETURN FARES (Third Class) |
|---|---|---|---|---|---|
| | | | | a.m. | s. d. |
| BURTON-ON-TRENT | ... | ... | ... | 10A33 | 7 9 |
| DERBY (Midland) | ... | ... | ... | 11 25 | 7 6 |
| BELPER | ... | ... | ... | 10†40 | 7 0 |
| AMBERGATE | ... | ... | ... | 10†46 | 7 0 |
| WHATSTANDWELL | ... | ... | ... | 10†51 | 6 6 |
| CROMFORD | ... | ... | ... | 10†58 | 6 3 |
| MANCHESTER (Central) ... arrive | | | | 1 5 p.m. | ... |

"A" Passengers change at DERBY in each direction.
† Passengers change at CHINLEY.

### RETURN ARRANGEMENTS

MANCHESTER (Central) depart :—
    4.32 p.m. for DERBY and BELPER only.
    5.50 p.m. for all stations (Cromford, Whatstandwell, Ambergate and Belper passengers change at Matlock).
    7.35 p.m. for all stations except Burton-on-Trent.

For Particulars of facilities from Matlock Bath, Matlock, Darley Dale, Rowsley, Bakewell, Great Longstone and Monsal Dale, see separate announcements.

---

**HOW TO REACH THE GROUND**—A frequent 'bus service runs from PICCADILLY to MAINE ROAD.

---

CHILDREN under three years of age, free; three years and under fourteen half-fares.

---

### CONDITIONS OF ISSUE

Day, Half-day and Evening tickets are issued subject to the conditions applicable to tickets of these descriptions as shown in the Bye-Laws and Regulations, General Notices, Regulations and Conditions exhibited at Stations, or where not so exhibited, copies can be obtained free of charge at the Station booking office.
For LUGGAGE ALLOWANCES also see these Regulations and Conditions.

---

### TICKETS CAN BE OBTAINED IN ADVANCE AT STATIONS AND AGENCIES

Further information will be supplied on application to Stations, Agencies, or to W. B. CARTER, District Commercial Superintendent, London Midland Region, DERBY. Telephone: Derby 2442, Extn. 204.

November, 1951                                          BR 35000

A. Gaunt & Sons (Printers) Ltd., Heanor, Derbyshire.

Designed & Printed by Swannack Brown & Co. Ltd., 13a Anlaby Road, Hull.